Life Worth Living

From Lithuania to Boston
My Journey of Building Resilience

LUBA SAKHARUK

First published by Ultimate World Publishing 2020
Copyright © 2020 Luba Sakharuk

ISBN

Paperback: 978-1-922497-32-1
Ebook: 978-1-922497-33-8

Cover design: Ultimate World Publishing
Layout and typesetting: Ultimate World Publishing
Editor: Rebecca Low
Photos: Cover top photo Nadia Clifford, Digital Transformation Coach, LeapFrog Systems. Photo taken from the 41st floor of One International Place, Boston MA. **Cover bottom photo** Luba Sakharuk, December 30th, 2019 Copyright License: suesse-Shutterstock.com

Ultimate World Publishing
Diamond Creek,
Victoria Australia 3089
www.writeabook.com.au

ULTIMATE WORLD
—— PUBLISHING ——

What friends and colleagues had to say...

"I do not remember how and where we met, all I know is that I do not remember my life in America without Luba. My family and I moved to the States in the early 90s, when I was 15 years old. During the first year, my life felt like a survival challenge as I was living in a foreign country, going to a high school with a very different educational system, and trying to communicate in a language that I did not know. Although every day back then was very stressful, I remember walking to and from school with Luba, talking to her for hours, taking dance classes together, and going to fantastic birthday parties that she organized so well. I always had a feeling of hope that everything would be okay because I had a friend like her.

Through all the challenges of immigration, I don't remember a single time when Luba complained or was discouraged. Her positive personality attracted many people, creating a large circle of friends, and making everyone feel included and wanted. She made friends and stayed friends with them by giving so much of her time and heart to people.

After we left for college in different states, she kept in touch with me throughout the years in the same effortless and positive way that was characteristic to her. As we graduated from college, lived in different states, found jobs, got married, and had our children, and through all the expected ups and downs of life, I still don't remember a single time when Luba complained about anything. Now, as an adult, I appreciate her optimistic energy and am at awe of her ability to see the positive side of every situation. So many years later, I still feel that everything will be okay because I have a friend like Luba in my life."

Irina, a friend since 1992

"We met too long ago to recall all the details of our first encounter. I do remember that I was a senior and Luba was a freshman in high school. In high school, a three-year gap in age is huge by all means but we became instant friends back then and I am still thrilled to call Luba one of my closest friends now.

Regardless of the many ebbs and flows of life, Luba has always been a beacon of inspiration and support for me. For my friend, everything was a glass half full, even when there were just a few drops in that glass. Luba's life has not been easy or without bumps, but her attitude towards life has always been optimistic and uplifting for the past 28 years of us knowing each other.

Luba's positivity and seeing things, events, and people from an ever-optimistic, level-headed, and reasonable angle have always been there. Luba has that innate ability to see the best in everything and everyone around her and I have always found that so inspirational and admirable."

Ilona, a friend since 1992

"I've been lucky to know Luba as a friend and a colleague for many years and have witnessed her spirited life journey through some of the biggest highs and lows. Even in the toughest situations, her compassion knows no bounds and I have been truly inspired by her calm, stoic, and fearless approach to life throughout our friendship.

She's the most optimistic person I know, and I cannot imagine anyone better suited to write a book about a positive mindset."

Oleg Vitsev

"Luba is a woman that always leads with a positive mindset. She doesn't say 'yes, but' she says 'yes, and'. She is not only a born leader and mentor but also a sincere person who is passionate about her work and her team. She has a gift of being able to motivate, engage, and enhance a team. In our work environment at a small company, stress levels were always high. We all know that stress can bring out the worst in people, but not Luba. She brought all her values and practices into our workplace and taught us all how to achieve greatness using positivity and mindfulness. It was her insistence that we pursue these approaches that helped us grow into a productive and accomplished team."

Joy Darby

"Luba is a wonderful coach and a friend that everyone should have. She has an extraordinary ability to direct tough situations into collaborative teamwork. She has helped me with two of the most difficult obstacles in my life. With her hopeful outlook on how she handled her daughter's cancer diagnosis, it helped me to face my reality with courage and strength. Luba has an innate, sweet nature and sees the good in any circumstance. As a doctor, I tend to plan for the worst-case scenario and am critical of others. With her gentle guidance and encouragement to filter the negativity, I have started to develop a special lens for the pleasant, optimistic, and constructive outcome. It has helped me to navigate my work and personal life with joy. Luba's book reminds me of the times we spent together and inspires me to stay positive. When life gets hard, I will remind myself Luba can find the pearls, and so can I."

Jenny Chang, DMD, DMSc
Harvard School of Dental Medicine, 1997

"Reading the 'Life Worth Living' book brought me back to my teenage years. I have known Luba Sakharuk (Yelovich back in the day) for over 30 years. We were inseparable for a few years before she emigrated. At some point in our lives, both of us living in new countries and facing many life challenges, we didn't talk that often and didn't exchange letters, but the bond we formed earlier was too strong to break. Once I came to the US, we picked up exactly where we left off. While I still lived in Vilnius in the mid-90s, I remember Luba coming to visit, always bringing presents, and taking us out to eat at restaurants. She would bring something carefully picked out for everyone. I didn't realize it then, but now I understand how hard she worked, earning minimum wage to be able to afford not only the airline ticket to come to Vilnius, but all those gifts, each picked out with high attention and love!

One of her trips to Vilnius was especially memorable for me. She worked all summer to earn enough for the trip and the airline lost one of Luba's suitcases. It was full of gifts. I remember her being on the phone, trying to figure out what was going on but the luggage was never found. She was heartbroken. She was very upset. With that said, there were no tears. She kept it cool, counted her losses, and moved on. The funny thing was that even with one luggage being lost, she still managed to have enough in her hand luggage to give at least something to everyone. I talk a lot here about presents but it was not the gifts that made our friendship special. It was the fact that Luba truly cared. Attention and love are what made our friendship last so long.

As I read the book, I realized how much of Luba's pain I wasn't aware of. With all she went through, she didn't get harsh or depressed. The opposite, she remained an attentive and loving mother, wife, daughter, sister, and friend, always finding the right words to support and cheer you up. She continues to enjoy giving and being a kind person. The book talks about how many challenges life can throw at you, how many sacrifices a family might go through, hard decisions having to be made, and having enough strength and coping mechanisms to not give up. The book encourages you to stay positive, kind, and grateful for all and everyone you have in your life. I am grateful for having met Luba many years ago and for our friendship. I am thankful for everything she has done for me and the priceless life moments we have experienced together. I wish Luba the best of luck and success in her life journey, as well as her new journey of being an author!

**Aliona Tchumanov,
a friend since the late 80s!!!**

This luggage, full of snacks and presents, summer's worth of work at Stop & Shop never made it to Lithuania ☹

Dedication

To my beautiful daughters, Elena and Anna. You are only teenagers now, but it is already clear you are both amazing people with compassion and kind hearts. You may have different personalities and even different interests but the sisterly bond you have is forever! Cherish it!

I am too grateful to only have a single dedication, so here is dedication #2

To my aunt Manya, who had the courage to bring not only her sister to the US but the whole mishpacha (aka משפחה, family, семью)!

To my grandparents who survived World Word II and raised my parents to be caring and selfless people.

To my parents who gave us what they could and raised us the best way they knew how. You guys did a pretty good job if I may say so myself!

To my sister, who is brilliant in everything she does and has been there for me all my life. You mean the world to me.

To my husband, who believed I could accomplish more than I could have ever imagined myself. You turned out to be an amazing dad as well! Bonus!

To ALL who have touched my life, thank you for being you! Keep feeding and spreading kindness!

Contents

Foreword

When life gives you lemons, you write a book. That is Luba's life in a nutshell in 2020. This book is a fascinating memoir, but it is also so much more. It is a jigsaw puzzle of bits and pieces that make up who we are - flickers of memories, shards of pain, moments of reflection, bits of loving-kindness. It is a guide to a stronger, more resilient self. It is a map to a better life.

I am Luba's slightly older and (on a rare occasion) wiser sister. With the exception of our mother, I have known her the longest of any living person in the world. While she has many praiseworthy qualities, if I were to describe just one thing that makes her special, it would be her phenomenal ability to easily and organically build strong and lasting relationships. Her network of friends, extended family, colleagues, and acquaintances is vast, geographically distributed, and forever growing. One would expect that it would be impossible to have deep connections with so many people. After all, many of our relationships, formed at the time of rapid change and social media, are superficial and shallow and fade as quickly as they appear. Yet, Luba, with her empathy and positive outlook on life, manages to create bonds that (though often characterized by occasional and infrequent interactions) withstand the test of time.

Is it a blessing or a curse? One could argue that such a natural ability to connect to people—quickly and on a deeper level—is a practical soft skill that comes in handy in a wide range of personal and professional situations. However, being a good friend and confidant to a person, being in their inner circle and privy to their personal challenges, also often exposes her to their pain and loss. For someone who is not a medical, mental health, or social work professional, Luba has witnessed quite a few tragedies in her social network and helped numerous friends and acquaintances deal with difficult situations - without the benefit of professional detachment. While Luba does not divulge the details of such interactions, she will share on occasion that yet another friend is dealing with a loss or going through a difficult time.

Over the years, I pondered on many occasions whether it was worth it and whether her ability to relate and emphasize was causing her too much pain. But, I have also witnessed her growing stronger and more resilient, taking pain and anger—whether her own or witnessed through her interactions with others—reflecting on, learning from, and transforming them into something else. This book is, in part, about how she does it. Luba creates a powerful narrative by weaving in stories that are deeply personal to us both (though we often remember or interpret them somewhat differently) and turns them into examples and lessons in courage, resilience, caring, and healing. One such example is particularly worth mentioning as we both experienced it but from different perspectives.

I still remember my first-grade "audition", though the details have become blurry over the past 40 years. At six, I was a proficient reader and could recite a number of poems from memory. The elderly teacher was pleased. "This child I am keeping in my classroom", she said. As it turned out, another teacher greeted me on September 1st that year - a young, pretty woman, barely out of teacher's college. We became fast friends, as much as a teacher and her young student could be. Over the next three years, I could do no wrong. I was sad to leave her and kept going back to visit for several years afterward. So, when it was my sister's turn to enter first grade, my favorite teacher was excited to get another me in her class.

Luba's older (and on a rare occasion) wiser sister Ella

Except, of course, my little sister was not me. Though she had strengths that would be exalted as soft skills today, she did not meet the preset expectations of the teacher. Excitement quickly turned to disappointment. "The difference between you and your sister is like the difference between heaven and earth." This casually dropped sentence from an overall good and decent person had become a knife that cut deep into a child's psyche, eventually healing over deep emotional scars. For the next three years in elementary school (and to a lesser extent in later grades), Luba recalls being compared and ultimately not measuring up on regular bases. She uses this story to raise awareness of how our words might negatively impact others, even inadvertently (as was likely in this case), and so much more so when delivered with malice.

I never saw the scars. I saw a happy child, always surrounded by friends. I saw an always smiling young woman, reaching and surpassing her goals in life. I saw an accomplished and talented engineer, agile coach, facilitator, mentor, manager, and leader with scores of glowing recommendations on LinkedIn. I saw a supportive wife to her husband and a loving mother to her children. In the book, Luba doesn't talk about years of self-doubt and self-imposed low expectations during her formative years. Yet, as she admitted much later, this particular incident was the moment that filled her with self-doubt and was when she stopped reaching for the stars. It took years to remediate the damage. While this experience could have become a self-fulfilling prophecy, I believe that it was also a pivotal event that significantly contributed to who she is today.

Luba often says that her own lived experiences, however formative, seem trivial when compared to the tragedies, trials, and tribulations of our grandparents and great grandparents. While history books are often too far removed for us to fully relate to the enormity of the recounted events, my sister and I inhaled and absorbed first-person accounts by the survivors of the Holocaust, famine, poverty, repressions, and persecution. These stories were often told as a matter of fact - the horrors to be remembered but left in the past. Three generations later, these experiences are very much a part of our identities. The strength of our grandparents (all of whom are now gone) continues to shape who we are. But, our own lives are full of lessons that should not be underestimated. We live in the age of rapid change, drive-through relationships, and skewed priorities. We are bombarded by unsolicited information, full of confusing, conflicting, and often negative messaging. How do we remain strong? How do we remain positive? How do we live the best life possible, a life worth living?

This book is a guide to learning from the past and the present. It has already made an impact. As Luba was writing it, she asked several friends and family members to read drafts at various stages and to give feedback. While the feedback was overwhelmingly positive, many said the book made them cry and reflect. Throughout the writing and editing process, the book also made Luba and I revisit many stories told in our families, and reexamine many memories and "truths" we had always "known", giving us a better understanding of people and events that contributed to who we are today. These particular stories might not have been part of your journey, but the goal of this book is to make you laugh, cry, reflect, and learn from your own experiences - those that make your own life worth living.

Ella Eptheyn, EdD

PART 1

Family

My parents, Sofiya and Efim!

It all started with this signature in 1973

Mom Sofiya, little Luba, adorable Ella and dad Efim

Luba

Ella

Luba

Ella

6

Introduction

"There are only two ways to live your life. One is as though nothing is a miracle. The other is as though everything is a miracle."
—ALBERT EINSTEIN

I will begin with full disclosure that I have had a very happy childhood. I was loved by both parents and grandparents, I never experienced hunger, I was never domestically abused and I haven't experienced any real-life tragedy. Well, at least not firsthand. I will now knock on wood and spit three times over my left shoulder, just in case...I don't know if this stuff works, but no way am I taking any chances!

My life so far has been...it is very hard to find just one word to describe it. Maybe this could be something the reader can help me choose after they are done reading this book. In this book, I share stories that might make you smile, stories that might make you cry, and stories that might make you think and rethink your own experiences and your actions. Readers might find the book educational and maybe even inspiring. This book is a memoir, so I am hoping my children, along with my nieces, nephews, and children of the many first, second, and many times removed cousins I have all over the world, will find it interesting at some point in their lives. I am also hoping this book can impact people who are looking to have a more positive outlook on life. I don't have a certificate in Positive Psychology or a degree in Neuroscience. I do, however, happen to be one of the lucky people who see good by default, even in the worst situations. I don't know what causes some people to get that in their DNA, but I do know it makes life much easier. I also know that many psychologists and neuroscientists have done a lot of research and have published many studies on how you could actually rewire your default way of thinking. You are not stuck. You just have to want to change.

I ask that if you find a certain section too sad, too boring, or just not of interest to you and you catch yourself judging the book too much, please self-reflect, realize that someone has poured their soul into sharing their life story, and just skip to the next section. There are plenty of stories to choose from in this book!

Lastly, you will see the word "Babushka" used a lot in this book. I use it interchangeably with grandmother or grandma throughout the book and chose to keep this Russian word for two reasons. One, it is what I am used to saying when I talk about my grandmothers and second, it seems to be the one Russian word that most of my American friends know and get a kick out of saying out loud.

Sit back, relax, and enjoy!

CHAPTER 1

Finding Courage

"You will face many defeats in life, but never let yourself be defeated."

-MAYA ANGELOU

From a very young age, we are faced with unknown circumstances that we may find scary or extremely overwhelming. It may start with taking your first steps (if not earlier) and it never stops. When we are young, we think that all of our troubles will go away when we finally become adults but boy, we are delusional.

There is a term I use that might not sound ladylike, but it gets the point across very well. The term is a **"LIBRARY OF CRAP"** or a **"LIBRARY OF PUNCHES"** if you are into boxing and not so much into borderline swearing. We accumulate this library. We hear stories from our parents and grandparents. We face our challenges and over the years, we broaden our horizon of extremely unpleasant situations. We accumulate our "**LIBRARY**" and we compare our new experiences with what we have already faced. If the new thing you must face is nothing compared to what you already have in your library, you get over it and move on. If you are facing something much worse than anything you have seen, heard, or experienced before, you add it to your library, knowing that it will make you a lot more resilient to whatever else life decides to throw at you.

In this book, I share examples of my library as well as the libraries of those special to me. These examples cause me to reflect and ponder on how in the world my relatives found the courage to face what life threw at them. The stories I share helped develop the courage and resilience in me that helped me cope in some pretty crappy situations.

How was I able to just add it to my library of punches and move on with my life without getting defeated? Keep reading to find out!

THE EARLY COLLECTION OF LIFE'S PUNCHES – OVERCOMING INSECURITIES FROM NOT SPEAKING ENGLISH AND GETTING MY FIRST JOB!
Introductions:

Me: Luba (short for Lyubov, which means Love in Russian). I am a 42-year-old female who was born in Vilnius, Lithuania in 1978 and came to Boston on September 30th, 1992. I often get compliments on my sexy accent...Well, I say sexy, others mainly just notice that I have it.

My siblings:

- Sister Ella. Met on the day I arrived home from the hospital. They say she was an adorable 2.5-year-old toddler. No way to prove it now!

- Half-brother Arkadiy. My father's son from a previous marriage. Met when I was 9 years old and he was 16.

I was never that child who got straight As and was on top of all the school work or chores. I was a good kid and if my dad asked me to wash the dishes or sweep the floor, I would not dare say no to him. But, my parents didn't actually ask much of me. They never cared about report cards and there wasn't much of a structure when I was growing up. I was always well-fed (my dance teachers back in the day might have argued I was fed too well) and there were enough clothes to look as decent as the rest of the kids I knew. For some of my friends, there were rules like you come home, wash your hands, change out of your street clothes, eat, do your homework, and only then you could hang out with friends. In our house, there was none of that. I never had to force myself to do anything hard.

As I went through immigration, things changed somewhat. Perhaps that is when my happy and naive childhood began to transition to reality, but I still didn't see my life as a difficult one. Yes, I was made fun of on a few occasions in school because I didn't speak English and I cried into my pillow pretty much every night for the first 3 years, but I wasn't forced to study hard or work more hours than I signed up for myself.

I was extremely happy when I got a job at Stop&Shop packing groceries. The pride of that first paycheck I got at the age of 14 a few months after coming to the US was stronger than any job promotion that followed. Prior to getting that amazing first job, I had gone to countless ice cream shops and restaurants around the Coolidge Corner area in Brookline, MA. I even filled out an application at the CVS on the corner of Harvard St. and Beacon St., but besides a phone call from the manager who asked me if I wanted to go out on a date, there was no interest in hiring me. I still have no idea why a decent looking guy in his mid-20s would ask a 14-year old, who could barely say a few words in English, out. I understand he wasn't planning on discussing politics or solving world hunger with me, but still, wouldn't you want to have ANY conversation before whatever your intentions may be? I know...I know...I am 42, but I can still be extremely naive at times. He didn't seem all that creepy, but that phone call sure was. The only thing I managed to reply to him (in broken English with that very thick Russian accent that many of the readers would know from any American action movie with bad Russian dudes in them) was, "I have boyfriend." No, it is not a typo...I didn't forget about an "a." That was all I knew at the time.

I got very close to getting a job at an ice cream shop, but when the manager asked me to bring my social security card, I didn't know what it was. I had it, obviously, but because I didn't know what he was asking me, there went that dream job.

When I went to school sick, it wasn't because I was forced, it was because I didn't have a parent who spoke English who could call the school and tell them I wasn't feeling well. My sister Ella, on whom I relied for countless things growing up, attempted to do that on a few occasions but obviously, that didn't fly because she wasn't an adult. We even tried to explain on the phone that our mom didn't speak English, but you know how it is...rules are rules. I didn't want to get an unexcused absence, so I felt like I had no choice but to suck it up and go to school.

School #6 in Vilnius, Lithuania   **Brookline High School**

For the first two years of high school, I had this constant fear of someone asking me something in English and me not knowing what they were asking or not being able to answer and the whole class would be staring at me. One particular time, I entered the class and noticed that one of my classmates who was Russian and spoke much better English wasn't there. I debated if I should leave or find the courage to stay. I stayed. I tried to stand in the back of the class hoping that nobody would pay attention to me. No such luck. My dance teacher, Lynn, who ended up being my absolute favorite teacher in high school and continues to inspire me to this day, turned to me and said something. She was smiling, so I knew she wasn't pissed at me, but it didn't make it easier, so my heart sank. Thankfully, the Russian girl showed up and rescued me. She translated that I should be wearing a different kind of shorts for dance class in the future. Easy to say I thought. Someone donated two boxes of clothes for me and my sister when we arrived in America. I wore what I had. There was plenty for us to wear, but we didn't get to choose, and it was very unlikely that I would find a pair of shorts that my teacher would approve of. I shared part of that story with Lynn many years later. I shared how uncomfortable she made me feel when she spoke to me and we even laughed a bit about it, but I didn't share with her that finding training outfits and buying costumes for performances wasn't very easy, at least not in the first year. Sometimes, even when we mean well, we are not aware of how our actions might affect someone. With that said, Lynn and her dance lessons made my high school years so much more enjoyable.

PONDER: When you interact with someone who doesn't speak English very well or doesn't speak it, what goes through your mind? Do you get annoyed? What can you do to make it easier for the person you're trying to communicate with?

Based on my experience, BEING LOUDER DOES NOT HELP!

> **The following might be helpful (only if the person truly doesn't speak English. If they speak well but just have an accent, the following could be borderline insulting):**
>
> - Speaking slower
> - Using very simple words
> - Pointing to objects
> - Finding someone who can translate
> - Putting it in writing so the person can use their dictionary
>
> These days, Google Translate along with other translation tools is a blessing!

GETTING PAST THE FEAR OF FAILING
Introductions:

My husband: Timur. Met in September 1996. Got married on April 29th, 2002. Very smart. Very educated. Super hard working. Almost always right. No, really, he is!

Vlad: Friend who also studied at Northeastern and was my husband's roommate. He was also the best man at our small wedding in Hawaii.

My first, or perhaps the first memorable, encounter with having to actually "suck it up and do it" was when I was in college. Looking back now, 24 years later and all that happened over the years, it seems very minor, but since it influenced my life in a very significant way, I will share it.

To impress my now-husband after meeting him at Northeastern University in 1996, I decided to switch majors and transfer to the Computer Science department. I had to choose between a Bachelor of Science or a Bachelor of Arts in Computer Science. I really had no idea how it would affect my future, but the difference was physics classes! A Bachelor's of Science required three of them and it didn't

Luba and Timur, April 29th, 2002

sound appealing at all! Let's just say that physics was never my strong subject. I had no idea what programming was about but that somehow didn't scare me. "The less you know the better you sleep," I guess. I did always like math and that was the convincing factor. I had enough confidence in my math skills to make the jump, but boy did I dread those physics classes. My very smart husband who was my main advisor and mentor at the time, suggested that I should just embrace it. He was pretty sure that a Bachelor's of Science was the way to go and that I would do just fine. Still not sure why he had the confidence in me, but I had so much respect for him, I trusted his guidance. I imagine the fact that I was very much in love had something to do with my desire to impress him too. To be clear, since the last couple of sentences are in the past tense, I still have a lot of respect and love for my husband. I figure it is good to confirm since he will eventually read this book. The one thing that changed over the years is that I no longer try to impress him. This is the difference between 18 and 42. I don't try to impress anyone anymore. I am being me and if I happen to inspire someone, great. If not, that's okay.

I took those damn physics classes (apologies to the husband and my younger daughter who love physics very much) and guess what? I survived just fine. I didn't shine. I found the courage to ask for help and I asked for help a lot. I didn't want to come across as dumb in front of my boyfriend, he had enough on his plate helping me with Computer Science classes, so I turned to our roommate Vlad who was extremely patient with me. I got Bs (Vlad could only do so much, after all, he wasn't a magician). The funny thing was, I actually enjoyed some of the classes, too. Inhaling the helium from a balloon and speaking in funny voices never gets old! Now, it is a distant memory. I haven't used physics since then and don't remember much of what I learned, but there was a very important life lesson there. Don't be afraid of the unknown. It might be hard, and you might feel like an idiot here and there, but you will learn and that will be it. I got over my fear of failing and it wasn't nearly as bad as I anticipated.

PONDER: What is it that you want to do now but afraid you won't be good enough? What would be the first step to overcome that fear? What is the absolute worst thing that could happen if you gave it a shot and it didn't work out? What will happen if you don't try? What will happen when you embrace it and succeed?

Embracing this unknown put me on a path to the career I love. I don't do anything physics related or even programming now for that matter. I do, however, wake up every morning grateful to have found my passion. I get to connect with hundreds of people in many different companies and help them transform organizations. I get to inspire and influence people into changing the way they work to achieve great results. I get to watch the "aha" moments in not only organizational changes on a large scale but also the small transformations in the way people see their contributions to a larger purpose. Whatever you decide to take on, even if you decide that it isn't really your thing, finish it. It will give you that feeling of achievement. You will have that extra confidence. You will stand a little taller. You will have additional respect for yourself. You will learn something new and you might find yourself on a path you didn't even imagine.

WHEN ATTEMPTING TO BE A HERO BITES YOU AND OTHERS
Introductions:

Me: Someone who really doesn't like letting others down.

In my career of over 20 years now, there was only one time that I took something on that I didn't actually deliver. If there were others and I don't remember, it is probably because feedback was given, I learned from it and I moved on. I remember this particular experience because I let people down and they ended up scrambling at the very last minute to change direction in what we were supposed to deliver. We never talked about it after, I just wasn't a part of that team anymore. I held on for too long instead of being honest and telling them earlier that I was overwhelmed, exhausted and that coding a project in Java was not coming together. What I learned in that scenario is that you must be honest with yourself and others as far as the load you take on.

Don't be afraid of the unknown, but don't be a hero either. If something isn't going well, communicate. If you have to deliver bad news, prolonging it doesn't make things easier in the end, only the opposite. It is not easy to find the courage to ask for help and it is not easy to find the courage to deliver bad news. However, it is better to find that courage than to live for years with the regret of letting someone down. I know some of you may think, "What about those people that could not care less?" I have to be honest, even though there might be a few bad apples out there, most people don't want to let their colleagues down. I have had many coaching sessions with folks and if you base your feedback around how their actions impact their co-workers or even better, common goals or outcomes, for the most part, people care and want to do the right thing.

SIDE NOTE: I know some people have an immediate gag reflex when they hear words like a "positive mindset", "mindfulness", "rewiring your brain", and anything related to changing their personality. Many refer to it as "touchy-feely stuff." You can't help someone who doesn't want to change, and I don't attempt to change anyone in this book. With that said, for those who would like to learn more about how to change, I highly recommend looking up Daniel G. Amen, M.D, as well as the book called Personality Isn't Permanent by Benjamin Hardy, Ph.D.

STORIES OF MY FAMILY'S LIBRARY OF LIFE PUNCHES
Introductions:

> **My parents:** Sofiya (also known as Sofa or Sonia) and Efim (Fima).
>
> **My father's side of the family:** Bezrukov/Yelovich.
>
> **My mother's side of the family:** Lopert/Slavin.
>
> **Grandparents** on my **father's side:** Antonina (Tonia) and Lev (also known as Liova and Leiba). Tonia's maiden name was Bezrukova. Tonia's married name was Yelovich (Jelovic in Lithuanian).
>
> **Grandparents** on my **mother's side:** Anna (also known as Nyusia, Hannah, or Anya) and Solomon (also known as Semion and Monia). Nyusia's maiden name was Lopert. Nyusia's married name was Slavin.

Grandparents Tonia and Liova

Grandparents Monia and Nyusia

Liova's mother (my great grandmother), Sheine (maiden name Skuder) Yelovich with her father Yechiel ~1910

My great grandparents, Grandfather Monia's parents, Sofija and Emanul Slavin, Mogilev 1903

CHOOSING WHAT TO FOCUS ON

Seven years ago, my babushka Tonia just came back from visiting my dad at the hospital. He had had another stroke. It happened just before his 66th birthday. They would call each other at specific times to make sure they were both okay, but this time he didn't pick up the phone. There were no other family members left in Vilnius. My grandmother was 92 and she was the only one taking care of my dad, though at that time despite many health issues, he still lived somewhat independently.

After he didn't pick up the phone, she immediately knew something was wrong and went to check up on him. She found him unconscious and called an ambulance. It wasn't his first stroke, it was his third or fourth. It seems odd that I can't remember how many strokes for sure my dad suffered, but I don't. They were spread out over 25 years and there is no record of medical history available besides old pieces of loose paper that I found a few years ago. No doctor could tell me much either because they just recently started to computerize their systems in Vilnius and none of the systems in various hospitals are connected. Regardless, each time he had a stroke he became weaker and recovery took longer. Babushka didn't think he would make it that time. She spent a lot of time at the hospital with him and even though he survived and regained his consciousness, he was in his own world, saying things that made no sense, and he wasn't responding to questions. When I spoke to her on the phone two days later, she described his state of mind and it was heartbreaking. I, unfortunately, witnessed it following yet another stroke last year. It was very difficult to watch and I couldn't help but think about my grandmother being all alone the last time it happened.

When my dad had his stroke in 2013, she had just come home from visiting him and was in the kitchen when someone rang the doorbell. She didn't expect anyone and there weren't that many people left who knew her, let alone those who came before calling first.

My dad, in the kitchen on Uzhupio St., when he was still able to walk without a walker, 1995

She opened the door and found her neighbor's son-in-law, Andrei, standing there. A few years back, Andrei had given a tour of Vilnius to our family who lives in Israel, so they knew his phone number. My dad's brother Misha moved to Israel in the early 70s with his wife Rimma and little Kobi, my cousin.

When my grandmother saw Andrei, her first thought was, "It is not possible, I just saw him at the hospital a couple of hours ago."

Misha, Fima, Liova, Tonia

Misha playing accordion

Dad's brother Misha and Misha's wife Rimma

21

Misha, his wife Rimma and my dad Fima standing. My grandmother Tonia, little Kobi and my grandfather Liova sitting.

"Sit down auntie Tonia," said Andrei. She knew he had bad news for her, so she braced herself for the worst. "It is not Fima...it is Misha in Israel," said Andrei. This was on October 2nd, 2013. I don't know if our relatives from Israel couldn't reach grandma and so they called her neighbor, or whether they wanted to make sure someone would give her the news in person, but it was Andrei who ended up telling her that her older son had passed away. My grandmother was not a very expressive person. She wasn't into hugs, kisses, and cuddling, but she had a huge heart. Her heart broke at that moment.

It was 7am Boston time the following day when I spoke to her. I was standing in front of 270 Congress St in Boston, about to start my workday. I got a message on Skype from Andrei's wife Leila that my dad had a stroke and Misha had passed away, so I called her as soon as I got off the train. Neither my dad nor my grandma ever embraced calling the

US. If they needed to get in touch or wanted to check-in, they would call one of my friends in Vilnius who would skype me and I would know to call. I would also randomly call to check in on them, but I have to admit, probably not as often as I should have.

This time, Tonia didn't sound like herself. There was so much pain in her voice that all I could think of was how much I wanted to hug her. I offered to come right away but she refused. My sister had bought tickets already but grandma was adamant Ella didn't come. With my dad barely alive, she wanted to focus on him. She was very stubborn at times and I didn't fight her on this. I didn't want to add stress. So, at 92, without much support, she had no choice but to find the courage and embrace the fact that she just lost her older son and was possibly about to lose her younger son as well. I often wonder what helped her stay strong at that particular moment. At some point, she said something along the lines of, "I cannot help Misha now...but I can still help Fima." She was in tremendous emotional pain but chose to focus on what she had at least some control over.

PONDER: When something extremely painful happens to us, what can we do to cope? When parents lose their children, where do they find the strength to move on? When one loses their sibling, how do they cope with pain? What about a close friend? A parent? A spouse?

Musicians might turn to music and produce the most heartfelt songs that many can relate to. Many people focus on other family members, knowing they have to be strong for them. Many use writing to heal. Some start cleaning or focus on house renovation. Some sell everything that reminds them of their old life and move. Unfortunately for some, alcohol and drugs become the go-to. Unfortunately for others, tragedies create more tragedies.

> When you see a homeless person, do you ever wonder what their life story is? What happened? Do you immediately judge or look for ways to help?

THE LIBRARY OF PUNCHES GOING MANY GENERATIONS BACK - POVERTY, LOSS, HUNGER, PRISON, HARSH PUNISHMENTS, RESILIENCE

Introductions:

Tonia's parents: Maria and Andrei Bezrukov.

Tonia's grandmother on her fathers' side: My great-great-grandmother **Daria**.

Tonia's siblings: sister Anna, brother Nikolai.

Tonia's nephew (sister Anna's son): **Boris Zubarev** (now 82 years old and lives in the village of Sokol, my grandmother's birthplace).

While writing this book, one memory led to another and I learned some additional facts about Tonia's side of the family. There was so much pain and loss over the years, her own library must have been loaded. Often, when I have to face a challenge, I think about what my grandmother encountered over the years. I wonder if she often thought of her grandmother, Daria. Her father's mother, Daria, had 16 children, out of which only six survived into adulthood, five sons and one daughter. Here is a picture of her, along with her son Andrei and his wife Maria, my great grandparents.

My great-great-grandmother Daria with son Andrei and Andrei's wife Maria

A Russian author, Valerij Kosariov, wrote a book in 2015. The book is about love and the pain of World War II and is focused on the people from this small village of Sokol and the neighboring village Dudenego. He describes not only my family members, starting with my great-great-grandmother Daria, her children, and their spouses, but talks about many of the neighbors and people my grandmother had mentioned in her stories. He describes the pain, hunger and the harsh punishments of that time. He shares a story of one young teenager who was imprisoned for five years because he took three cucumbers from a field. My grandmother Tonia's brother-in-law was sentenced to seven years in prison after the war already ended because he took a flyer they weren't supposed to read out of someone's hand and got caught. It took three years for him to prove his innocence while his wife assumed he was gone and remarried.

The author describes a scene between this man, Nikolai Petrovich Zubarev, and his nine-year-old son. The man asks which of the boys is Boris Zubarev. When the nine-year-old replies that it is him, Nikolai introduces himself as his father. Boris was my grandmother Tonia's favorite nephew and was a huge part of her life until the very end.

FINDING WAYS TO COPE - THE HAPPY PLACE

From 2013 until May 2017, my dad and my grandmother Tonia lived together in a small 2 room apartment on Uzhupio street in the old town of Vilnius. My grandmother had lived there for 70 years. My dad could no longer live alone. He was

Boris with his wife Nina

able to talk, eat by himself, and actually regained enough strength to walk with a walker. That alone was a miracle. But, he didn't leave that apartment for four years. His change of scenery consisted of moving from his bedroom to the bathroom where he could wash up, then walk using his walker to the "living room" where my grandmother slept. He would move from one room to the other. He sat on the couch and watched TV. He would do some physical therapy exercises throughout the day, move slightly to get from the couch to the dining room table three times a day, and by 6 pm, he would relocate back to his bedroom. Every. Single. Day. For four years.

Not to digress, but when the COVID-19 pandemic hit and we all had to be quarantined, thinking about my dad would give me enough perspective to count my blessings and just enjoy the everyday activities such as cooking and the ability to go for a long walk daily.

He dreamed of going back to his small house (dacha) just outside the center of Vilnius. He loved his dacha so much, he talked about it constantly. When I came to visit, he drove my poor grandmother and I nuts! I truly believe that it was the hope of going back there that kept him sane. It was his happy place.

**A few moments captured
in mid 90s at our dacha,
my dad's happy place**

FINDING STRENGTH WHEN YOU HAVE NO CHOICE
Introductions:

> **Babushka Tonia:** Resilient, courageous, loyal, and strong are just a few ways to describe this incredible woman. Always taking care of someone. Always doing chores and running errands non-stop.
>
> **Jolanta:** A woman that came into my dad's and grandmother's life as an angel in disguise in 2015. She helped them with everyday chores that my grandmother, being in her mid-90s, was finally willing to delegate to someone. Jolanta's big heart, her honesty,

and her desire to help others had no limits. I will be forever grateful to this woman for everything she has done for us.

On May 9th, 2017, after five weeks in the hospital, Babushka Tonia passed away from cancer. I was with her. A couple of hours before she passed away, she said quietly, "Soon…" She knew and she was content. She had spoken about and planned for her death for a few years and at 95, she was ready.

Saying goodbye to my grandmother, as difficult as it was, was only the beginning of a series of life punches I would have to block or embrace. I dreaded coming home after she passed away and having to tell my dad that his mother, his only caregiver, was gone. He took it better than I expected, which was a relief. I think he suspected she wouldn't be coming home. The next challenge was deciding what to do with my dad. My sister researched all the possible ways to actually bring our father to the States but he wouldn't even consider it. His worst nightmare was to be a burden. I completely understood.

"Gemma" is the name of a very high-end nursing home in an area of Antakalnis in Vilnius. It ended up being his home for the next two and a half years. I promised to visit him very soon because I had to go back to the US.

I came back for his birthday a few months later. Besides visiting him and potentially trying to find a different arrangement for him, I had another task. I had six days to clean out my grandmother's apartment to rent it out so we could pay for my dad's stay at Gemma. She had lived in that apartment for 70 years. That place had history. She raised her kids there, she took care of her mother there, she lost her husband there and it was the place I had visited not only weekly for the first 14 years of my life, but many times in the 25 years since we left. It had the same furniture, the same dishes, the same clock that appears in every family picture taken in that apartment. I had six days to empty it. All the dishes, all the

**Luba with grandmother Tonia
at the Uzhupio apartment**

**Dad Fima and
grandmother Tonia**

Sister Ella with grandmother Tonia

closets, and the furniture. I had to watch people carry out the bed my grandmother slept on for 70 years. That bed was an antique.

As grateful as I was that somehow, with a lot of help, I managed to find the people willing to just come and take it, it was painful to see it being carried out. It wasn't just the memories of my grandmother, it was the memories of my great-grandmother Maria who spent the last 5 years of her life there. It was the stories about my grandfather Leiba who slept on it. It was me spending two weeks there when I threw my back out so badly, my grandmother had to attend to me my whole two-week stay. It was the memories of my older daughter sitting on the bed when she was 14 months old and again when she was nine years old. The sweetest memory of all was of my younger daughter Anna at two months old with my grandmother Tonia, sitting on a chair next to her, smiling and playing with her tiny little hand. Her neighbor Galia was there as well. As I was watching these two women having the time of their lives with this tiny bundle of joy, I remember looking at my grandmother's happy face thinking, "It wasn't an easy trip with a two-month-old but it was so worth it."

SIDE NOTE: Here is another memory that took place in that apartment. A FUNNY ONE! It has to do with a little sneaky 14 months old, who is now 14 years old and gave me permission to share this story. She was potty trained very early on. We brought a cute, yellow portable potty, with us. At some point, she figured out that if she sat on it long enough for her cute butt to stick to it, she could then quickly get up and make the potty flip in the air, landing with a smash and a good laugh from Grandma Tonia. She didn't do it when Grandma Tonia was busy in the kitchen. She waited for her undivided attention and repeated that comedy act many times during the week. It didn't fail once. The audience found it amusing each time. In fact, Grandma Tonia would remember that visit over the years as the one that brought her a ton of joy. It is the little things in life, right?

Those six days were, by far, the most difficult days, both physically and emotionally, that I have had to this day. Nothing could be compared to the experience of opening every drawer, every box in the back of the closet, finding a bag with a red cross on it from World War II, and pictures from my grandfather's funeral that I have never seen before. Reading the final letter my grandfather wrote to my grandmother to say goodbye before he passed away was heartbreaking.

Liova

Liova, Fima, Misha, Tonia

That six-day experience alone made me resilient enough to handle the next challenge that came my way.

Where did I find the strength? What made me resilient enough? What was going through my mind during those six days?

I didn't keep a journal, so now this is all from memory. I remember crying a lot but then wiping tears off and going to the next shelf. I remember having a horrible allergic reaction from the dust, popping allergy medicine, and grabbing a bucket of water and a cloth to wipe the dust off. I remember looking at a few shelves I had cleaned and feeling accomplished. I remember feeling like if I was able to get through those, then I would be able to continue with the rest. I remember being grateful for having Jolanta in my life, a woman who knew my grandmother and helped my dad tremendously when I couldn't be there for him. She helped to find a home for many of the items and carried a ton out. Knowing that some of my grandmother's clothes or curtains that had been on those windows for as long as I remember could bring someone else joy made it easier for me. Storing some of the stuff at Jolanta's house made it emotionally easier as well, even if she threw them out herself.

I knew it was what I would have to do eventually anyway, so why not get it over with? I knew that by cleaning out the apartment, I would help the girls that really wanted to move in since their apartment next door didn't have working heat. At the same time, renting it out would help financially with my dad's care. I felt like I had no choice but to plow through it. So, I did. I can plow through anything now. I know that. I don't want to, but if given no choice, I will.

PONDER: What was the most difficult thing you ever had to do in your life? How did you manage to get through it? What did you learn from that experience? What did you learn from that experience about yourself?

WHEN CANCER STRIKES, NOT FINDING COURAGE IS NOT AN OPTION
Introduction:

> **My mother's cousins:** Edik and Arkadiy.
>
> **My great aunt Manya (grandmother Nyusia's sister):** The woman who came to the US in the late 1940s and made it possible for my family to come to the United States in the 1990s.

I could write a separate book on how cancer affected my family. Cancer is everywhere these days. Day in and day out, I hear someone getting diagnosed. At first, it was my great aunt Manya. It was the first time someone I knew closely faced it. We visited her at the hospital when she told us she was diagnosed with cancer. I remember looking at her and thinking, "No big deal, right? They have a cure, don't they?" It didn't really sink in. When we came to visit her shortly after at her house, I remember her saying, "I would take 5 years. 5 years would be great. I have so much still to get done."

I never asked her about her exact diagnosis or stage of cancer or prognosis. When I stopped by to see her after a couple of months, the decline was so rapid, it was scary. It started to sink in and I didn't know how to cope. I kept going full speed with my life, thinking I would go visit the next day. Or the next day. Without meaning to, I removed myself from the horror of watching someone you care about suffer from this horrible disease.

Years later, my mom lost her sister Lena and cousins, Arkadiy and Edik to cancer. All three lived in Boston and we would see each other on birthdays or some random occasions.

When my great Aunt Manya passed away, I was in somewhat of a shock. I was in denial. I couldn't believe it happened so quickly, or so it seemed to me. When Lena, Arkadiy, and Edik were gone, I was sad. But, when it happened to my Grandmother Tonia, I was truly heartbroken. I still am.

It is easier with time, but when you wake up in the morning thinking I should really check on my grandmother and my dad to realize in less than a second that they are no longer there, the pain is still there. I know it gets easier. Time does heal. You never forget though. Not when it is someone you truly cared about.

When my 14-year-old daughter got diagnosed with cancer, what I felt was something I cannot describe with one word. The best way I can describe it is getting on a very scary roller coaster which starts to drop down and you get that knot in your stomach, except the knot stays for weeks until you learn that the cancer hasn't spread and is highly treatable. Not finding courage was not an option.

COPING WITH WHAT MAY SEEM UNBEARABLE

My 14-year-old girl was perfectly fine when she had her physical on February 27th, 2020. She got a flu shot that day, so when she started coughing the next day, everyone thought it was just a flu shot side effect. When the cough continued after two weeks, I took her to Urgent Care. They didn't hear anything in her lungs and said the cough was a side effect and it would eventually go away. Another week went by and the cough got a little worse, but she could still sleep fine through the night. She was a lot more tired than usual though. Another few days and her lower back started to hurt. Another day and her upper back started to hurt, though she was still able to go for a nice long walk. Another day went by and she could barely walk with me, she had to lean on me to get home from the walk and was out of breath. I took her to an emergency room.

In the emergency room, they tested for the Flu (A and B), Strep and did a chest X-ray. They saw a bit of water in her lungs and said it was most likely the beginning of pneumonia. They gave her antibiotics and sent us home. 30 minutes later, they called us back and said the ER doctor just looked at the X-rays and wanted us to come back for a CT scan. We came back and within half an hour, we were looking at a mass, a tumor

34

that looked like it took up a third of her lung. Our pediatrician arranged for us to go to Boston Children's Hospital. They waited for us, met us by the car with masks, and walked us straight into an isolated room where doctors and nurses were already geared up with special gowns and masks. The Covid-19 pandemic added to the scare. After 10 hours and having seen many oncologists, they moved us to the oncology floor. The next two and a half weeks were excruciating.

PONDER: How does one find the courage to keep on going when their child gets sick? What choices do parents have when their kids get sick?

Many people asked me how I managed to cope. The question I asked back was, "What choice do I have?" I didn't know how to get rid of that knot in my stomach or how to not be scared. I did eat a lot of ice cream because unfortunately, I am a stress eater. It didn't help much though.

I actively reviewed my library. I went through all that happened in the lives of my great-great-grandparents, my grandparents, all that was still happening around me, and the possibilities of what could have been. Shortly after we arrived at Boston Children's Hospital and I was in the right state of mind to ask questions, we found out the tumor was outside of the lung. This was actually a relief. I thought of my Babushka Tonia who took care of her sick son for over 25 years. I thought of her strength when she chose to focus on the son that was still alive after finding out her older son just passed away and being completely heartbroken. I thought of a friend whose son relapsed and was about to get a bone marrow transplant. I thought of my close friend who is living with stage four cancer for which there is no cure.

It didn't take long before I started counting my blessings. I chose to focus on what I had control over. I chose to be there for my daughter who was about to start a very unpleasant journey of treatment. I chose to keep a journal and write about this journey. Writing was healing for me. It occupied my brain and channeled my energy towards something more worthwhile than just stressing out. I chose to keep friends and family updated so they worried less. I chose to care about friends, family, and my daughters. I decided to take it one day at a time. Finding courage may be difficult, but it is not impossible. We all have it in us. We just need to choose what works for us.

What works for you?

_____

_____

_____

_____

_____

_____

_____

_____

_____

_____

_____

CHAPTER 2

Giving a Damn

"Being unwanted, unloved, uncared for, forgotten by everybody, I think that is a much greater hunger, much greater poverty than the person who has nothing to eat."

-MOTHER TERESA

Introductions:

Nina: Family friend. She is my dad's age and lives in Vilnius. Her mom and my grandmother Tonia were best friends for many decades. She was there when my grandmother was admitted to the hospital. She was there when she had her surgery. She was there for my dad, waiting for me to arrive from the US. She was always there when they needed her. She always cared. She still does. She checks in with me regularly to make sure we are all doing okay.

"Thank you for not abandoning us," says my father with a deep appreciation in his voice.

I am sitting across from my dad in my grandmother's small apartment on Uzhupio St. in Vilnius, Lithuania. It is April 2017. He doesn't look unhappy or depressed. His walker, which he uses to get to the restroom and a small bedroom where he goes for the night, is next to him. He isn't able to get into the kitchen with it because the door isn't wide enough. He used to be an amazing cook and would spend most of his free time in the kitchen, but those days had been long gone. He seems to be truly appreciative and grateful for me being there. I am his little girl that "came to the rescue" when they needed me the most. He doesn't know yet that his mother, who is 95 and who has been his primary caregiver over the last 25 years, is dying from stage four cancer.

The four walls of that small apartment, TVs in both rooms, and my grandmother Tonia had been his world for the last four years since his latest massive stroke. Once in a while, a family friend Nina would visit and they had recently let a nice woman, Jolanta, help them out a little around the house. My grandmother would tell me over the phone that there was this amazing woman that came into their lives that could actually wash laundry by hand as well as she could. I loved that about my grandmother. She was always super neat, always running around doing chores. All her life, she refused to install a washer because no way it could wash as good as she could by hand. She had her standards and she stood by them!

Jolanta and Nina were a big part of my dad's life when my grandmother passed away. He always looked forward to their visit and they never disappointed him. There is no doubt in my mind that they truly cared for him. They both showed they gave a damn by their actions. Rain or shine, they would visit my dad, bring him his favorite snacks and give him the best present of all, their time and companionship.

CHOOSING TO CARE UNTIL THE VERY END
Introductions:

Maria Bezrukova: Babushka Tonia's mother. Passed away two weeks before my mom and I left Vilnius to come to the US.

Misha Yelovich: Tonia's older son.

Rimma Yelovich: Misha's wife.

Misha's and Rimma's children: Yael and Kobi (in Russian, it is Yasha, in English it is Jacob, but even Grandma Tonia referred to him as Kobi after she visited Israel).

When my father thanked me for being there, I was a bit shocked. I didn't see myself doing anything heroic. Why wouldn't I come? I grew up with people around me showing me what giving a damn looks like. I don't know any other way. All her life, Babushka Tonia took care of someone. She was in her early 20s when she married my grandfather and moved to Vilnius, Lithuania from Russia. She was in her early 50s when my grandfather passed away.

Tonia and Liova looking at each other with love and admiration

He had been sick for a while and according to my grandmother, he probably had lung cancer, but it was not diagnosed back then. When she was in her 60s, she took care of her mother who was sick with Alzheimer's.

My great-grandmother Maria Bezrukova lived in the village called Sokol all her life and suffered a stroke when she was around 90. My grandmother Tonia still held a job as an accountant when she moved her mother to Vilnius. She juggled work and taking care of mom for a few years until my great-grandmother became bed-ridden

39

and my grandmother was forced to retire. I still remember visiting my grandmother's work when I was a little girl. She was very loved and very respected there. She would often tell stories about how much she loved her job and how she looked out for the younger employees, mentoring them and just simply re-doing some of their work because their numbers wouldn't add up and she didn't want them to get in trouble with management. She loved her grandchildren and her great-grandchildren. She loved her sons. Her love was not a smoochy and fluffy kind. She came across as cold and strong, but if you knew her, you would know how deeply she cared.

She would often talk about her son Misha and his wife Rimma. She had a lot of respect for Rimma and often expressed her concern about how hard Rimma worked. She would remember her trip to Israel to visit them and how much it meant to her. Misha always cooked and so he somehow managed to cook up a storm for a surprise party without having my grandma get suspicious. She would often talk about that party, expressing her excitement as far as how many people came. She loved visiting relatives and sightseeing. It was a special time for her. She felt bad she couldn't visit Israel more often after my dad got sick, but she did what she had to do. She felt she had no choice. But, the choice was there, she just chose to give a damn and do what she felt was right. I know she loved Misha and his family. She knew that Misha was

surrounded by his wife, kids, and many grandkids, while my dad was alone. Alone and sick. She didn't have it in her heart to leave him, even for a couple of weeks. She did everything for him. I remember being absolutely amazed by her, even when she was approaching the end of her life.

She cared so much and wanted to spare my dad's feeling so she refused my offer to take her home to die peacefully in her own bed. She cared with all her heart all her life and was choosing to do so until the very end.

Tonia

40

MAKING GESTURES THAT ARE MEANINGFUL TO OTHERS
Introductions:

Boris (short is Boria) Zubarev: Tonia's nephew.

Nina Zubareva: Boris's wife.

Marina: Boris's and Nina's daughter.

Masha: Boris's granddaughter, Marina's daughter. Since Boris was my dad's cousin, it makes Masha's mom Marina and me third cousins, which makes Masha my niece a couple of times removed. Masha is just a super amazing relative.

Yael and Kobi: Uncle Misha's kids from Israel.

Arkadiy: My half-brother. My dad's son from a previous marriage.

On the day of my grandmother Tonia's funeral, while already at the cemetery, my newly-met relative Masha (short for Maria), who came all the way from Nizhniy Novgorod for the funeral, came up to me to ask a question, "I brought some soil from Sokol, do you

Marina with her daughter Masha

think it's okay if I throw it in the ground after the casket is lowered?" Masha was my niece; Boris's granddaughter. She was named after Grandma Tonia's mother Maria. I had met her Grandfather Boris, Grandmother Nina, and mom Marina when I was a young girl. They would come to visit regularly and relatively often, and I heard so much about them from

Babushka Tonia that it felt like I had known Masha all my life. I was so grateful that she came.

Grandmother Tonia with her dad Andrei and her sons, Misha and Fima

Saying "goodbye" to my grandmother, planning the funeral, worrying about how to get my father to attend the funeral, and figuring out how to provide around-the-clock care for him, while having a life over 4000 miles away across the ocean, was overwhelming to me. Masha had brought many photos of her grandparents and of the house in that village, Sokol, where my grandmother grew up. As I watched my dad smile, while looking at those pictures and remembering details of the house and garden and how the furniture was arranged, I could see it brought him a lot of joy. He had visited his grandmother Maria at her home a few times over the years, but the journey wasn't easy and as far as I remember, he had not gone there much after my sister and I were born. Babushka Tonia, however, went to see her mom often. Whenever I was in Vilnius, my grandmother and I would stay up late talking. She would tell me her childhood stories, how exceptional her mom was, and how huge her dad's heart was. She would tell me about her mother's washed floors and stacks of crepes all done by 6 am before the rest of the family got up. She told me about their amazing garden and the friendly neighbors and her trips.

As far as the question from my niece Masha is concerned, I admit I might be a lot more nostalgic and sentimental than others, but the question about soil from Sokol brought tears to my eyes. I was holding it together pretty well up until that point, but that act of kindness just overwhelmed me. She didn't have to come at all, and she sure didn't have to bring the soil from the place that was so special to my grandmother. It was a selfless act that was an example of giving a damn.

My dad was able to make it to the funeral. It wasn't an easy task, but we somehow managed. His late brother Misha's kids, Kobi and Yael, along with Yael's son and boyfriend flew in from Israel for the funeral. It was the first time I met them, but all those late-night talks with grandma and pictures she showed me made it feel like I knew them. My dad's son Arkadiy also came and so we had four men carry my dad in a wheelchair (that we had to frantically find, rent, or borrow) down two flights of stairs. Whatever grey hair I already had at that time had to have at least doubled as I watched sweat pouring down their red faces. Talk about being under pressure, right? They brought him back up the same way after the funeral and it felt like I exhaled for the first time that day.

PONDER: What have you ever done that was extremely meaningful to someone else? What did it mean to you? What did it mean to the other person? What made you decide to do it? Was it part of a larger goal, or did you do it just because you knew it was important for someone? Does the "why" matter?

When we choose to do something for someone else, we might have different reasons to do it. It might be because it makes us feel good and we are not even thinking about how it might affect or impact someone else. It might be that we thought really hard about what we could do to make someone's life or situation a little easier or better. Sometimes we think we are doing it for someone else but in fact, that person could not care less. Sometimes, we choose to do something nice because we know someone is watching. Regardless of the reason, we should strive to do good in the hopes that whoever is watching or experiencing it will be inspired to do the same.

My cousins Kobi and Yael, along with relative Masha

PONDER: What does giving a damn mean to you? Who inspires you to be a more caring person? When was the last time you showed someone you give a damn? What could you do for someone tomorrow? Next week? Next month? What is stopping you? When leading by example, who would you inspire to do the same?

When I tore my ACL in 2019 in an unfortunate ski accident, my daughters showed how much they cared and wanted to help. They alternated between bringing me ice and food. I remember thinking how grateful I was for having such amazing kids when my older daughter brought me a plate of cheese, pears, and chocolate and asked me if there was anything else I needed. I don't normally pat myself on the back, but I remember being proud, giving myself a little bit of credit for leading by example and showing my kids what my parents, grandparents, and my uncle Valera showed me when I was growing up.

Leading by example and showing what kindness looks like affects people that surround us. It is not enough for us to read a book, get inspired, and then do nothing. Giving a damn doesn't cost anything. Showing someone that you care, in the hopes that they will then pass it along, goes a long way. It is important. We can all do it.

WHEN ONE'S SELFLESS ACT CHANGES THEIR LIFE FOR THE WORSE

Introduction:

Me: a teenager having to make a very difficult decision.

My dad: a loving father who also had to make a difficult decision.

My mom: a loving mother in the middle of unexpected circumstances.

My sister: a 16-year-old who was never away from her family, now in the United States, feeling alone and depressed.

Nyusia: our mom's mother.

As far as selfless acts go, here's a memory of one that caused much pondering over the years. It is a memory of my dad letting me go to the US. To this day, I debate in my head if it was a selfless act or an act of the least resistance. Something that happened in his life prior could have been caused by a similar behavior, but the connection occurred to me only recently. I may be overthinking it, but I could never understand how he could have a son from a previous marriage and not see him from age one (or so) until 16. My dad wasn't a jerk. He was a very loving and caring father. He was a great guy with a big heart. He wasn't selfish. As the story goes, he made many attempts to see his son, even brought a present for Arkadiy, but according to my father, it wasn't accepted by my dad's ex-wife and was thrown down the stairs. This was the only story or explanation that I could ever get out of my grandmother. I never asked my father about it. I don't know what happened to cause that relationship to fall apart, but my dad and his ex-wife were only married until Arkadiy was one. Dad's ex-wife must have been a very strong woman who thought having her new husband adopt Arkadiy would be better for the boy. Did my father just simply comply? How much fighting for his son had he done before giving up?

45

Arkadiy was two when my parents got married and as far as my mom remembers, my dad didn't visit Arkadiy from that point on until he came to visit us at the age of 16. I remember that visit. His little sister came with him as well. I remember my mom being very welcoming and we all had a blast. At some point, we even went on a small vacation with just our dad, Arkadiy, my sister Ella and I. I wish we had captured at least one picture. Glad I have it captured at least in my memories. Arkadiy and I met many times in Vilnius since that first visit. He looks exactly like my father which is both a little creepy and heartwarming! I am grateful to have met him. I am guessing here...but I don't think one could have too many siblings!

To me, my dad could do no wrong. I had always chosen to see our somewhat messed up family as a result of different circumstances and not blame anyone. Blaming does not change anything, and it doesn't make difficult circumstances easier. Talking about difficult circumstances and analyzing lessons we can learn from them does help, but more about this in the next chapter.

Here is a memory from 1992. I'm 14 years old. I'm still in Vilnius. I'm standing in some official building and there's a piece of paper in front of my dad. I still remember what my dad looked like at that moment and I remember his eyes, full of sadness and concern, looking into mine. He is young, healthy, and has no grey hair, it is a bit thin on his forehead, but it doesn't make him look less handsome. He's supposed to sign a piece of paper and give my mom permission to take me to the United States with her. He looked at me, holding the pen in his hand, and asked, "Are you sure?"

Here is what went through my mind. I am 14. I need to choose between going with my mother to an unknown (to me) country very far away where they speak a different language or staying with my dad, whom I loved unconditionally with all my heart. I was very close to my mom; she was and still is a great mom, but I was daddy's girl. Here is another factor I had to consider at that point. I haven't seen my sister for a couple of months already. Babushka Anya, Uncle Val, and my sister Ella have left for Boston a few months prior. Ella, who was 16, didn't expect how difficult it would be away from her family in the new country. Nothing could prepare her to be away from mom. I often wonder if Babushka Anya, having gone through what she went through at 17, which I describe in detail in the next chapter, couldn't really understand my sister. Everything is in comparison after all. However, what my sister experienced at 16 couldn't be discarded as nothing just because others experienced things much worse.

My mom, at least back then, was not a very strong person, not physically and not emotionally. For me to not go with her would just completely crush her. I wasn't aware of what my sister was really going through at the time. I only remember one time, Ella calling our house, talking to my mom, and crying uncontrollably. For my mom not to get reunited with Ella when Ella needed her so much was not an option. Getting my sister a ticket to come back was not an option either. Once she got on that plane, there was no turning back. I don't know what the paperwork would even look like in 1992. I don't know anyone who decided to leave in the 90s and then returned shortly after.

My dad seemed extremely strong to me. He was this big guy that I looked up to and I didn't think there was anything he couldn't handle. The guy could fix everything, from a refrigerator to an open wound that needed stitches. Nothing fazed him. When, as an eight-year-old, I decided that jumping from the roof of a shed was a good idea, landing on a piece of glass and slicing my thumb, I ran straight to him. When, at the age of five, I somehow casually ran into an axe which was lying near the never-ending construction at our summer house (dacha), my dad looked at my shoe filled with blood and without even blinking, took care of the wound.

I had to choose between staying with my dad or going with my mom. On the surface, it was my choice, but it wasn't much of a choice. I had to go with my mother and I told my dad I was sure. He signed the paper.

Me and my dad during my first and second visit in the mid 90s.

What I couldn't understand at that point, but I very well understand now, is that signing that paper was equivalent to signing away a life worth living. It might sound extreme, but being a mother of two teenagers and watching their relationship with their dad, I can't imagine me taking the girls and leaving. I can't imagine taking them to a country far away and have him not know if he will ever see them again. I can't imagine him not having the ability to just pick up a phone and call, not even talking about Facetiming here, a simple phone call was not an option. I can't imagine him ever doing it to me either. How does one continue to find purpose in life after your kids, whom you love very much, are gone? Every time I would visit, he asked me to tell my sister Ella how much he loved her. Every. Single. Time.

He also often asked me if I heard from Arkadiy. Did he ever feel guilty?

Dad with my sister Ella

48

One could easily argue that he abandoned us. There are so many reasons why he lost his family, many of which are the consequences of his actions. One might see the situation of him sending a 16-year-old with her sick grandmother to another country as absurd. Without any financial or emotional support, my sister's future didn't look promising. She was heading toward deep depression and severe anxiety. It is hard to imagine what would have happened to her if our mom (out of bravery or whatever else was leading her) didn't pack her bags quickly.

My father never expressed any kind of regret. He usually expressed how happy he was that my sister and I did well and that our mother was happy. He never accused anyone of abandoning him. He didn't see himself as a victim, regardless of how it may have been perceived by others. Yes, he was sick later in life and so he was grateful I was there, but he never blamed anyone for what had become of his life. He did, however, express on a few occasions that he didn't have much of a voice when it came to decision making. "Nyusia ruled the family," he once said. This phrase caused a lot of pondering over the years. I dive a bit more into this topic in the next chapter.

SIDE NOTE: My mom's mom, grandmother Anya whose nickname was Nyusia was a resilient woman with a very strong personality. Most of chapter three is dedicated to her life story.

WHAT HAPPENED TO DAD AFTER WE LEFT

My dad had his first stroke before he was 50 and I found out that he was in a deep depression for a year after we left. When I came back in 1995, three years after we left, he wasn't one hundred percent healthy, but he recovered well enough to speak, walk and still drive. He met me at the airport in 1995. His health, however, continuously declined over the years afterward. The next few visits, he no longer came to the airport but waited for me at my grandmother's apartment (he didn't live there until much later). Then it got to the point where he waited for me at his place. For many years, my grandmother would cook food and bring it over for my dad, take his dirty clothes to her place to wash and bring them back to him. The trip would take over an hour each way, she had to take a trolley, then a bus, and then walk a mile on a dirt road. For years, while my dad attempted to live on his own at the dacha, our next-door neighbors would help him with the day to day tasks. This was their life for years.

SIDE NOTE: Our neighbor Nadia is now in her 80s and continues to take care of that small house (dacha). Her husband, for years, took care of the lawn and they both took care of my dad's dog Rex, his most loving and loved companion. I have known them all my life. When I say there have been many people in my life who lead by example and have shown me how to be empathetic and caring, Nadia, along with her husband are definitely among those people.

Rex was my father's best companion for 17 years

I am not sure what made my dad thank me for not abandoning him. He was grateful beyond words and he wanted to express his gratitude. What did he expect? Him signing that paper gave us an opportunity to have an amazing life. I don't know if, by the end of his life, he looked back and questioned if it was worth living his. I do know he found joy in little things. I can tell for a fact that I will be forever grateful to him for letting me go and to my mom for doing what she had to do.

SIDE NOTE: Over the years, my mom offered countless times to go to Vilnius and help take care of dad. For years, she continued to call Vilnius and check-in with Tonia. Although I had always admired her for her empathy, I always advised her against going to Vilnius. Knowing the living situation, the instability of my mom's health, as well as my dad's health and short temper (strokes don't help with that), I couldn't imagine it working out very well. My grandmother and dad seemed to have found a routine that worked for them. At times, although they were always happy to see me, even my visits threw them off and according to my grandmother, it took a few weeks to get back into the swing of things.

My dad didn't expect anything, he was just grateful that I came to be there for my grandmother. He was helpless and I, in return, was grateful that I was in a position to come. I was grateful for my husband who took care of our kids. I was grateful for my sister who was ready to hop on a plane or do anything I needed her to do. I was grateful that my mom became stronger over the years and was healthy enough to enjoy life. I was grateful that my workplace gave a damn about my family and allowed me to spend five weeks away from the office. I was grateful that for whatever reason, maybe it was the life circumstances or lessons we learned from our parents and grandparents, both my sister and I grew up to be decent people who choose to simply give a damn, every single day.

As mentioned earlier, this book is not about positive psychology or the science behind how being kind to others affects your own brain and happiness. I am sharing what matters to me, what makes me happy, and what makes my life worth living. I am fully aware that even though giving a damn comes naturally to me when it is about my family and friends, I know there is definitely room for improvement. I will continue to self-reflect and focus on that larger purpose in life. I know without a doubt that giving, whether it is financial or your time, directly correlates to a Life Worth Living! What is YOUR Purpose? What makes YOUR Life Worth Living?

CHAPTER 3

From Blaming to Healing

"Blaming things on the past does not make them better."
-NELSON MANDELA

We know blaming others doesn't fix anything, but it seems to come naturally to us humans. People turn to blame for different reasons, from covering up their wrongdoings to avoiding consequences to simply justifying some of their own behaviors or reflections.

For years, I blamed my parents for not raising me to be more confident. When I shared with my sister, way into our adulthood, how dumb I always felt because she was always the smart one in the family, she shared with me how ugly she felt because I was the pretty one. The fact is, our parents meant no harm. We are both average looking and although I still think my sister is simply brilliant, my confidence for sure has gone up since I was a kid. They didn't think of my sister as ugly and they didn't think of me as dumb. They meant to encourage us by telling me how pretty I was and telling my sister how smart she was. We interpreted their words our own way and so we both made assumptions.

Luba with sister Ella at Luba's 15th Birthday party, 6 months after coming to the US

What we say, how we say it, and actions we take might impact others in a way we might not even realize ourselves.

Here is a memory from September 1984. My first-grade teacher looked at me and said, "You and your sister are like heaven and earth." She had no idea that at 42, I would still remember her words, remember what she looked like when she said it, where she stood, where I stood, and how it made me feel. What I assumed she meant by those words was that compared to my genius straight A student sister who she taught for three years prior to taking on my grade, I was dumb. She didn't say I was dumb, but that's what I heard. There was no follow up of any kind. If at any point she said anything encouraging to me, pointing out some kind of talent I had, it is likely I would get over that statement. She didn't though. Of course, we can't control what people hear, but being aware of how your words might be heard is a step closer to not having a negative impact on someone. I don't blame the teacher now, but I did for many years. I would replay her laughing when she showed my mom an essay I wrote in the first grade with seven spelling errors in an eight-word sentence. It had a big fat F on it (one out of five on the old grading scale). I was seven years old. I felt ashamed. Think of any word opposite from smart and that is how I felt at that moment. Worthless.

The fact was, my sister and I were very different children. What I have learned over the years, however, that what I lacked in my ability to learn by sitting in one place and reading for hours, I made up with my personality and ability to connect with people. If I wasn't able to understand something technical from reading a thick functional spec, I learned by asking my colleagues to draw it on the board and explain it to me. What I also learned from being in IT since 1997 is that people who are extremely smart and educated enjoy explaining what they know to others. I became a good listener and so I learned regardless of what my teacher assumed as far as my ability to learn.

**Luba not looking too thrilled
on this beautiful day**

THE TOXIC ENVIRONMENT, ASSUMPTION MADE AND MEMORIES THAT STAY

Introductions:

Babushka Anya (aka Nyusia): Born in Ponevezh (Panevėžys in Lithuanian). Evacuated to Siberia at the age of 17 at the start of WWII.

Grandfather Monia Slavin: Born in Mogilev, a Belarusian city on the Dnieper River. Studied in St. Petersburg, Russia.

Yelena (Lena Slavin/Joffe): My mother's sister. I remember watching her give a kid a violin lesson when I was about 7. Unfortunately, shortly after, she became mentally ill and was heavily medicated for most of her life, until she passed away from lung cancer when she was in her early 60s. She remains one of the most beautiful and talented people I have met.

Rimma and Diana: My cousins. Twins. Yelena's kids.

Valera (Val): My mother's brother and my uncle.

Grandfather Monia, 1950

Grandmother Nyusia with
aunt Lena and mom Sofiya

Mom Sofiya on the
right, with dad Monia
and sister Lena

Mom Sofiya in the middle with sister Lena to the left and dad Monia

My aunt Lena

My uncle Valera

Cousins Rimma and Diana

Cousin Rimma

Cousin Diana

Great aunt Manya with cousins Rimma and Diana

I was lucky enough to have grown up with two grandmothers and one grandfather. This particular realization came to me later in life. I appreciate it now more than ever, watching my own kids and their love for my mother, the only grandparent they have truly known. My mom Sofiya has six grandkids and has been saying for years that she is the richest woman on the planet.

Sofiya with all 6 grandkids, 2011
Celebrating Elena's 6th birthday party!

My mother Sofiya and grandkids Anna and Elena. November 2017. Sofiya's 70th Birthday.

Grandma vising us for a weekend. 2019

This chapter, however, is not about my mother. It is mostly about her mom, my grandmother Anya, also known as Nyusia. She lived through a lifetime of trials and losses. This woman went through a lot. Her courage had no limits. One of the hardest that I witnessed was the loss of my grandfather Monia.

Grandparents Monia and Nyusia

I was 12 years old and I remember his funeral as if it were yesterday. I remember my grandmother hugging the casket and crying, "You left me all alone." I remember my mom trying to console her telling her she is not alone as she has all of us. Nyusia had to cope with a lot throughout her life and I don't know how she managed to live through it all, but when it came to losing grandpa, she chose to pack up and leave Vilnius. Everything reminded her of him and it was more than she could handle. She chose to finally reunite with her sister Manya in the United States.

Manya and Nyusia

After all the paperwork was done and their apartment was sold, the unimaginable happened. She went into cardiac arrest and nearly died. There was barely any time for her to recover, but it seemed there was no backing out at this point, so she, my sister, and my uncle Valera left for America.

My grandparents' and Valera's apartment in Vilnius. Photo taken by me during one of my visits to Vilnius

To me at 14, and for years to follow, it seemed as if my grandmother took my sister to America because my sister studied English and really wanted to go with her. To my sister, it seemed like my parents sent her away so that she could take care of Babushka Anya. In reality, the decision for my sister to go was made prior to Babushka Anya getting so sick. For Babushka Anya and Valera, there was no turning back. They sold their apartment and everything in Vilnius. Sending Ella with them, especially when Babushka Anya was barely alive, was a bizarre idea. Who was to blame? No one. Babushka Anya thought that if they took Ella along, then my dad and grandmother Tonia would follow and come to America as well. I doubt that in her wildest dreams she could imagine it not going according to that plan. Neither Babushka Tonia nor my father had ever even said out loud that they would never come. They went through the process of filling out paperwork and having the medical examination just like the rest of us, so assumptions were made and a lot of pain for many people in the family followed.

For years, I blamed my grandmother Anya for breaking up our family. There was some truth, a lot of truth, to my dad's words when he said, "Nyusia ruled the family," but she definitely wasn't to blame for the decision (regardless of who made it) to let my sister go to the United States without her immediate family. That decision impacted many lives. Some lives turned out pretty great (mine for sure) and some, not so much. Reflecting on why it happened the way it happened is helpful only if we extract lessons from it. One of those lessons was clear to me from day one. I would never separate my kids from their father. Another, I will never say anything negative about my kids' father to my children, my mother, or anyone for that matter. For many years, I assumed that my grandmother couldn't see the good in people or at least, the ability to keep the bad she saw to herself. In reality, I only knew what I saw. I was a kid. I had a limited view. I often imagined how many scenarios in our family would have played out differently if there was more open communication among my family members. It might be the reason why I am an open book now; too open one might argue.

I, as a kid, didn't blame but despised the fact that I often had to hear about how horrible my dad was. No kid wants to hear that about their parents, especially since even as an adult, I don't agree with what I have assumed for years was my grandmother's opinion of my father. I have many memories of my father taking care of my mom when she was sick, as well as my grandmother when she fell extremely ill two weeks before their departure to the US. I assumed my grandmother wasn't a fan of my dad, but according to my uncle Valera, who lived with Babushka Anya, that was very far from the truth.

Now that I have read many psychology books, I know that my grandmother Nyusia and my father were extremely different people. She had a very strong personality, while my dad was amiable. There had never been an open conflict between them and from what I remember, my dad never said anything insulting about my grandmother . I now know that there are so many perspectives and so many "truths" but my reality was, it was a toxic relationship where nobody openly said anything, but something was off. I grew up in this weird environment but since we didn't live together, I could visit for a bit and go home, leaving whatever that yucky feeling that I couldn't articulate was behind. I always came back though. At least a few times per week, I would go straight to my grandparents' place as soon as school was over. The smell of the most delicious cinnamon buns she would make must have been much stronger than whatever discomfort her words may have caused to me. She also had a huge smile each time she saw me. I am sure it was the same when my sister and my cousins came over. She loved us, no doubt. Grandfather Monia did as well. He had a huge heart.

SIDE NOTE: My grandmother Tonia would often say that Monia was a very honest and nice man. He was also very educated, but I was too young when we lost him, so all I remember is how extremely sweet he was to us grandkids. My cousins Rimma and Diana remember him a lot more, so it was nice to talk about him in the process of writing this book. He loved his grandkids. He didn't come across to us kids as someone who could have been a military prosecutor during the war. He was extremely kind and soft-spoken. I don't remember him ever raising his voice at anyone, although it is possible that he did, just not when I was around.

Regardless of the delicious cinnamon buns though, Babushka Anya's talking negatively about my dad behind his back made me somewhat resentful towards her. I never openly said anything to her. I was 18 when she died, so we never really got a chance to have a heart to heart. My mom and my grandmother would often point out all the wrong that my dad did, and I had to listen to it. I hated it. I remember being angry at both of them. Even as years passed by, that resentment lingered. Perhaps my mom had her reasons to share with her mother whatever bothered her. Perhaps it helped her through whatever she had going on. Perhaps my grandmother thought she was helping her daughter. People have their reasons and rights to say or do whatever they see fit. The lesson here, I suppose, is just look around and think about how it might impact those listening or watching.

I have plenty of good memories about Babushka Anya and I know she loved us, so I am definitely not blaming her for anything. As I learned more about Babushka Anya's life story, I could also understand her bitterness in the last few years of her life. I reflect and I try to understand so I can learn from it. I don't think empathy and gratitude are things that I learned from Babushka Anya. Not because she wasn't empathetic or grateful, but most likely because I never got to witness those qualities firsthand.

Nyusia in Brookline, ~1993

Nyusia smiling! ~1970

What other lesson did I extract from this particular story? To this day, when someone talks negatively about another person behind their back, I have a trigger that goes off right away. That trust that I may have had comes crashing down. It doesn't even matter if the person being trashed deserves it or not. It is how YOU talk about that person says a lot about you. If you have feedback for that person, say it to their face. Don't trash other people behind their back, it becomes a bad reflection on you. Another lesson, if you have something good to say, SAY IT OUT LOUD. SAY IT TO THE PERSON'S FACE. I do often wonder if my dad's decision to follow us to the United States would have been different had he been praised and appreciated more openly for all he had done for the family. It was not that easy to feed the family during the 80s and 90s. You couldn't just go to the store and buy whatever you wanted, even if you had the money. He had a huge garden with vegies, fruit trees and berries of all kinds. We had a large freezer in our living room and he would make the most delicious compotes all through the winter. He raised chickens and even pigs at some point. He built a homemade smokehouse at the dacha and would make all kinds of kielbasas and cold cuts. He would go mushroom picking, clean the mushrooms, dry them and supply even the most extended family. He would be up at 5am making breakfast for my sister and I before school. He was an amazing cook who found joy in feeding anyone who would stop by our house. Was he perfect? Absolutely not. Was there plenty to praise him for? Absolutely yes.

SIDE NOTE: According to my uncle Valera, my babushka Anya and my grandfather Monia, had the deepest respect for my father. In his memories, whenever they held family gatherings at their house, my dad would be the king of their kitchen and he and my grandmother were best buddies. It is scary how we can live all our lives having a certain perception, being one hundred percent sure it was real, when in fact, it might not be. I never heard my grandmother praising my father but apparently, he was praised a lot behind his back, just not when I was there. It is bizarre, after all that I have shared, but there are many memories of great family gatherings with lots of warmth and laughter. Somehow though, the few bad memories overtake lots of the good, leaving us heartbroken and in some cases, resentful for years.

PONDER: When you say something negative about your spouse, ex-spouse, son/daughter in law, co-worker, what outcome are you trying to achieve? Are you open to the possibility that doing so might not bring any value? Even worse, it might bring harm?!

It is always possible to look at each situation and come up with different interpretations of the story. I have always respected the fact that neither my father nor my grandmother Tonia talked poorly about my mother in front of me. Perhaps they waited until I wasn't around, but I will never know. Did they have a reason? Absolutely. One can always look at a fact and spin it whichever way they choose. Since there are many sides to a story, here are the sides that I imagine people knowing my family could come up with:

"My mother took the kids and left her husband."
"My mother took the kids hoping that her husband would follow along in a year or so, but he never did."

"My mother took the opportunity to give her kids a better life." ← That's a good one, huh?

"My father never planned to follow his family to the States because it was too hard and he didn't want to do it."

"My father couldn't abandon his mother, so he had no choice but to stay behind."

"It was all my grandmother Tonia's fault. If she agreed to come, my father would follow along and the family would be together."

"It was all my Babushka Anya's fault. If she hadn't decided to move to the US to join Manya and didn't take my sister with her, my mother wouldn't have to be torn between her kids and wouldn't have to follow her older daughter to the US, leaving her husband, who couldn't leave his mother behind."

If we were to get really creative, we could even blame Manya who has lived in the US since the 1940s because hey, why not?

Blaming is unfortunately a tendency that we humans have. As if it somehow takes away the pain you may have or solves a problem in any way. It does not. Not only does it not solve anything, but it is also somewhat pointless since you can't turn back the time. Also, you don't get a chance for a do-over and there is no way to know if a different decision would yield a better outcome. The only thing you can do is discuss, reflect, extract some good lessons, heal, and move on with life.

1992 turned out to be a very difficult year for many in my family. Babushka Anya ended up in the hospital as soon as they came to Boston, fighting for her life. My Uncle Valera still remembers the fear of the unknown and the emotional stress that came with immigration and a sick parent on top of it. While my sister was in the middle of her emotional pain, he was having a breakdown of his own, exhausted emotionally and physically from taking care of grandma as well as his job as a dietary assistant in the kitchen of a nursing home. I shared in previous chapters the pain that my father experienced when we left and what had become of his life after.

In comparison, my life in 1992 wasn't that bad after all...

Leaving aside the blame and choices that were made in 1992, **I choose to say I was given a chance at a future and I took advantage of it. I studied hard, I worked hard, and I am now living a *Life Worth Living!***

> **PONDER:** Is there anyone you feel strong resentment towards now? Are you in a position to discuss it with the person directly? If not, are you open to sharing your story with someone who could help see a different perspective? Are there any lessons you can extract for yourself?

SURVIVING THE HORROR AND STILL CARING ABOUT OTHERS
Introductions:

Nyusia (Babushka Anya): Evacuated to Siberia at the age of 17 at the start of WWII.

Manya (Nyusia's sister): Holocaust Survivor. Kovno Ghetto.

Nyusia and Manya's parents: Mordehai (Max) and Rivkah (Helena) Lopert. Lived in a small Lithuanian town called Anikshchai. They were both pharmacists. Rivkah was also a doula.

Larry: Manya's husband.

Misha Slavin: My mother's brother.

Babushka Anya was only 17 when she was separated from her parents and her sister at the beginning of WWII.

She was studying in Ponevezh (Panevėžys) while her sister was studying pharmacy at Kaunas University when the war started. As the family story goes...her cousin in Ponevezh (whom we later grew up knowing as Uncle Ylya) urged her to evacuate. She wanted to go home to her parents. "Do you want to go home or do you want to live?" he asked. They evacuated on one of the last trains out of Lithuania. This decision saved her life.

Imagine having to decide at 17 to get on a train in hopes of surviving when what you really want to do is hug your parents. Imagine making that decision knowing that your parents will most likely not survive.

SIDE NOTE: As the family story goes, they were killed by a Lithuanian neighbor. Someone they considered a friend. Someone Max had played chess with.

She escaped to Siberia from Ponevezh. She didn't speak Russian but she was fluent in Yiddish and Lithuanian. She didn't know if she would ever see her loved ones again. In fact, until the end of the war, she was pretty sure her sister Manya was killed. She didn't know that Manya survived despite living through the horror of Kovno Ghetto, followed by hiding in a small basement with 4 other people.

Once in Siberia, Babushka Anya was given a job in a daycare. There is a funny story about the kids using Russian swear words and the parents not understanding why she allowed it. They had no idea that Babushka Anya just didn't understand what they were saying. It is hard for me to imagine she didn't speak the language since, by the time I was born, Russian seemed to be my grandmother's first language. She had no accent, so I never knew she didn't grow up speaking it. Perhaps we were used to her accent. She used quite a bit of Yiddish and switched to it when talking to Grandfather. Grandpa understood but usually responded in Russian. In fact, she spoke many languages, the talent that I wished I had when I came to the US.

Back to her in Siberia. She had a job and she was at a place where they actually had food. Here is the most astonishing fact. She left Siberia where she was safe and fed and somehow made her way to Tashkent. The details of how she got there are now lost, but it is 2076 kilometers, which is 1849 miles, from Siberia to Tashkent. She went to look for her relatives. She found her mother's sister, Berta, along with the rest of the family on the verge of starvation. She didn't only make that long trip in the hope of finding them still alive, but she also brought food with her. I don't know what she managed to bring besides potatoes, but I know she continued to support herself and others. She was one of the most crafty women I have known. I remember watching her on many occasions sewing, baking, and knitting. I was told that she knitted and sold her crafts at a market to survive during the war.

She lost her parents at 17. Despite all she went through, she survived WWII and returned to her hometown in Lithuania after the war ended. She reunited with Manya but very briefly. They were separated again for 18 years and only got to see each other occasionally until we all moved to the United States in 1992.

Manya and her husband Larry, along with Babushka Anya, were supposed to leave Lithuania for Poland. They had a couple of days to make that decision when they were permitted to leave. The decision to leave Anikshchai led Manya and Larry to Italy. They later settled in Boston in the late 1940s. Babushka Anya chose a different route. The week they were supposed to leave, a handsome young man entered the town of Anikshchai with his Military Division. So handsome that one of my cousins recalled later that all her college friends had a crush on him when he was already a grandfather!

Grandfather Monia

Grandfather Monia was a military prosecutor. He was born and raised in Mogilev, Belorussia. He was one of eight children. His mother died during the birth of her eighth baby. His father, who was a school principal, did not have much. They had barely enough food but his father made sure that his children were highly educated. Details are lost now, but supposedly my grandfather wanted to become a doctor, but because it was considered more of a female profession (this surprised me), he settled for being a lawyer.

My grandfather Monia and Babushka Anya were married seven days later. Instead of sticking with a plan to leave with her sister, Babushka Anya chose to marry my grandfather and to become a military wife. Not an easy life. They constantly moved and lived in barracks. They had three children: my mother, her sister Lena and her brother Misha Slavin.

In 1972, tragedy struck. My grandparents lost their son. My mother lost her brother. While they were on vacation in Palanga, a resort town on Lithuania's Baltic coast, Misha Slavin drowned at a young age of 16.

Misha Slavin, late 1960s

> **PONDER:** How does a parent survive losing their child? Where does one find strength? How does one cope?

This goes back to the previous chapter. One finds a way to cope that works for them. I now unfortunately know more parents that lost their children. I can't imagine the pain they go through. I hope to never find out. I am sure life is never the same after a tragedy like this but somehow, they all have found a way to cope and continue to live.

When we were growing up, our mom never let us go near water. I remember I was embarrassed when I was in a summer camp because I was the only kid who didn't know how to swim. I didn't know what caused this fear of water in my mom until I was older. For some reason, nobody ever spoke of Misha Slavin. I remember finding pictures of a boy in my grandparent's photo album and not recognizing him. It seems my family wasn't into talking about their sorrows much.

SIDE NOTE: According to Uncle Valera, they all spoke about Misha, just not in front of him. My grandparents had no idea Valera knew he was adopted and so they didn't want him to find out. They were protecting him. They didn't want him to be hurt in any way. Valera, on the other hand, and the rest of the family knew about the adoption and until recently, I had no idea Babushka Anya continued to keep it a secret until the end.

Babushka Anya had a massive heart attack when she lost her son. Grandfather Monia, according to my mom, was never the same after. This tragedy affected the siblings as well. It is hard to say now if my aunt Lena's illness and my mom's health issues were a result of the stress, but I am sure it didn't help. I don't know what method to cope they chose individually. I am so grateful that out of all the ways my grandparents could have chosen to cope as a family, they chose adoption. They chose to care for someone and give someone a chance to have a home and a loving family. My uncle Valera was adopted when he was five years old. If you ask me, it was the best decision ever! I can't imagine my life without him.

Valera with Rimma and Diana

Valera with Luba and Ella

Valera with grandfather Monia

Valera with Luba, 1992 Brookline apartment on Winchester St.

Valera with sister Sofiya

SIDE NOTE: My most fun memory of Uncle Valera is when I was about five and he was asked to babysit my sister and I. He came over with his friends (they emptied the fridge, especially the salami that was very hard to buy) and we had the wildest party, jumping from couch to bed and back. It was a tiny studio apartment where my parents, my sister, and I lived until I was five. That couch and that bed were pretty much all the furniture there was. At some point, there was a closet that separated the bed, where my sister and I slept, from the couch that our parents occupied. My sister and I loved pretending we were asleep and then watching movies, peeking from the side of the closet so our parents wouldn't see us.

When it comes to giving a damn and choosing gratitude, Valera is a walking example. It is not just his loyalty towards Grandfather Monia and Babushka Anya and it is not just his loyalty towards Manya during her last days or my mom when she needs him. When I visited him and his partner and we went on a drive to the mountains, they said they had to make a quick stop. I was amazed when I saw many stray dogs run towards their car. Turns out, each time they drove to their house in the mountains, they stopped along the way to feed the homeless dogs. Their trunk was full of dog food and water. If this isn't the biggest sign of humanity, I don't know what is.

I mentioned earlier that I don't think I learned gratitude from Babushka Anya. Well, I definitely had my uncle Valera to lead by example. To him, Babushka Anya was someone who gave him a chance at life. He is one of the most empathetic people I know and when my sister, my cousins, or I would express how we didn't appreciate some of our grandmother's behaviors, he would remind us of the story of her life. He would remind us that she was an incredible woman who happened to have a very difficult life. Yes, there were some personality traits that we didn't appreciate, but if you looked for the good, there was plenty there. I choose to look for the good. Life isn't black and white. Life is complicated. I choose to learn. I choose empathy over blame and resentment. We decide for ourselves the kind of lives to lead and what our "Life Worth Living" looks like. You choose. The people you impact hope you choose wisely .

CHAPTER 4

Counting Your Blessings

"The positive thinker sees the invisible, feels the intangible, and achieves the impossible."

-WINSTON CHURCHILL

There is this misconception that positive people are always happy. I can assure you that even though I have a positive outlook on life, I get angry and sad just like every other human being. I can tell myself to "chill" or "screw the <fill in the blank>" but if that doesn't do the trick, I tell myself to "count my blessings".

SIDE NOTE: F*CK IT ALL (OR CHILL) STORY
My dad shared a story with me years ago, that influenced my outlook on stressful situations. It wasn't a funny story but it was about "chill" and actually became a joke between the two of us and later on among some of my co-workers. After his second stroke, he went to see his doctor. After a very thorough examination, his doctor turned to him and said, "Do you

want to continue to live?" "Yes," my dad replied. "Very well," the doctor said and proceeded to somewhat lecture my dad about keeping stress under control. He then told him to follow his exact directions, "Please take a deep breath and raise your right hand." My dad did exactly as he was told. Then the doctor said, "Now drop your hand, exhale and say out loud "Poshlo vsio na hui", which in translation really means "F*ck it all". The point was, that if you don't ever let go, you are not doing your mental state and therefore your overall health any favors. So, from that point on, if there was any kind of disagreement about any topic, without having to say a single word, one of us would just raise our right hand for a few seconds and drop it to the side. Message received.

I would like to acknowledge that no matter how much worse someone else has it, what you are going through may still be extremely painful and difficult.

Although my friend's son was at the Intensive Care Unit at the Children's Hospital fighting for his life and my daughter's Hodgkin's Lymphoma was highly curable, it didn't make it less painful to hear my daughter say to the doctor, "I know I am not going to die and I am not depressed. I don't have suicidal thoughts. I am just extremely sad because I am in pain and I am very weak. I was an athlete and now I am out of breath when I walk. I hate looking at myself in the mirror." What mother's heart wouldn't have clenched? I could have easily cried and got mad at the world or I could have counted my blessings and encouraged my daughter to be strong. So, I reminded her and myself that we were halfway through the treatment, her scans showed she was responding to treatment and that soon enough, it would just be a bad memory.

"If you can't control it, let it go," is a sign at the Jimmy Fund Clinic waiting area. Easier said than done, right?

I found this quote by Roy T. Bennett: "Count your blessings, not your problems" very inspiring and reflective of my approach to cope with painful punches life throws at me.

When things happen to us, it is very difficult to control the pain we are feeling or emotions that might take over. We are human and we are supposed to feel. The question becomes what you do about it. We can't control what happens to us but we control our actions.

When 2019 threw a bunch of painful punches my way, I decided to throw a few back and for every painful event, I challenged myself to find something positive. The next section is just that. A list of everything that occurred in 2019 followed by me accepting the challenge and listing all the great things that happened in 2019. It turned out to be very healing and much easier than I initially thought it would be. Let me walk you through that journey now.

THE PAINFUL PUNCHES OF 2019

January 2019
January of 2019 started with me coming down with the flu. The kind of flu when your temperature goes up to 103.9F (39.9C) and you don't remember much of the New Year's celebration at your home and your kids only see you briefly around midnight because you take enough medicine for the fever to drop down to 103 so you could walk down the stairs to wish everyone a Happy New Year!

February 2019
February 24th, while giving a ski lesson to a very cute 7-year-old, one of my ACLs was torn. No big deal. Nothing a surgery couldn't fix. Thankfully, it was my left knee, so I could still drive the kids around to ski races and dance practices. It was very painful for about 10 seconds and then it only hurt when I tried to step on it.

In the grand scheme of things, it was actually no big deal because I learned that one of my very closest and dearest friends was diagnosed with stage four cancer for which there is no cure. The emotional pain can't even be compared to the physical pain of the torn ACL. This was the second time in my life when cancer touched someone I loved who was my own age, but this was a different beast.

March 2019
I needed to schedule my ACL surgery.

My father who lived in Lithuania and had been sick for years had a brain bleed and needed emergency brain surgery. It was not clear what had happened because I was in the US and he was in Lithuania. It was not clear if he had fallen or had another stroke. It was not clear if he would still be alive by the time I got there. I needed to get on the plane that night because it was not clear if they would even do the surgery without consent from a relative. I bought tickets and headed to the airport.

I couldn't walk on my own much. I had a knee brace and could walk a little without crutches, but I could not straighten my knee and the overall physical stamina after the injury just wasn't there, so I requested a wheelchair service. The emotional pain of not knowing the state of my father was again, much larger than any physical pain at that point.

My father lived. No one could tell for sure what happened but it seemed to be another stroke. His ability to walk and eat by himself, which he worked really hard to get back after previous strokes, was gone. He only said "yes" and "no" and there were also signs of aggression when he screamed at the nurses and called them names. However, I was assured by the doctors it was still the anesthesia talking. In a few days, I found him in a hospital bed laying across the bed screaming that he just wanted to go...He couldn't articulate where just that he wanted to get out of his bed and go. I asked his nurses to help me put him back to bed. I didn't cry but my heart just ached for him. He was once a strong man who loved life and when asked how his life was, always answered

"The best!" It was always the best, even when the only way to get around for him was using a walker.

April 2019

I worried about the financial side of the very expensive nursing home where my father had lived for the last two years and would go back to post-recovery. I tried to sell the apartment I grew up in. There was no one left in Lithuania besides my dad and he would never be able to live on his own. We needed that money. It required a lot of paperwork. Most was done ahead of time while my dad could still give consent and I had limited power of attorney but that was not enough. There is a lot of bureaucracy in Lithuania due to many checks and balances to protect the elderly from being taken advantage of. Many government officials gave me this judgmental look like I was up to no good when I was dealing with the paperwork. In reality, I just wanted my dad to feel better, have peace of mind that I could pay for his care, and go back home to my kids and my husband.

I wasn't sure what to do about my surgery. My dad was very weak and no one could tell me if he would get better. If I had the surgery done and he didn't make it, I wouldn't be able to fly back to arrange a funeral. We decided my sister would arrange the funeral in the event our father passed away, but the thought of not making it to my father's funeral was haunting me.

I scheduled my surgery for April 12th and I was back in the US on April 2nd.

On April 4th, I got laid off from my job. Nothing dramatic. It was the right thing to do for the organization and I still think very highly of my boss and the company. I worked myself out of the job, which is actually a pretty awesome feeling. They were very kind and generous and allowed me to take the time for surgery and recovery. Regardless of the circumstances, however, it was an emotional departure for me. I loved the people on my team and loved my job.

On April 12th, I had the surgery done. The recovery was much worse than expected. Days two through five were the worst, but my attitude, for the most part, was, "This too shall pass. It is not life-threatening…"

At the same time, my dad was hanging on and my sister spent a week with him, making sure he got the best possible care. We don't know if he was even aware she was there, but to me, it was a relief.

September 2019 to December 2019

I visited my father four more times. October 1st was his birthday. He turned 72 in 2019. I brought a cake to his nursing home and he invited all the nurses to his room. One especially sweet one took his hands in hers, wished him a happy birthday, and asked if there would be dancing later on. He smiled in response.

He had lost a lot of weight since March and I watched him struggle to sit upright. His doctor suspected there was a chance he had lung cancer. My dad was too weak to get any tests done and regardless, he would not survive the treatment. It was just a matter of time now.

I saw him again in mid-November. He was unable to eat by himself. I continued to deal with the sale of the apartment, but at the same time, something told me I would not need that money to pay for the nursing home much longer.

The sale of the apartment fell through as the buyers failed to secure a mortgage. However, these people were still very interested in buying it and begged for more time to find an alternative. They needed two weeks to obtain a mortgage and asked me if I would come back. I caught myself feeling mad at them for not letting me know while I was still in the US so I could avoid the trip. Lithuania is not around the corner. Each time, there was jet lag and I was tired. Really tired.

Selling the apartment was no longer a priority. For multiple reasons, I could not say no. The buyers were really good people who knew my father and grandmother and even attended Babushka Tonia's funeral. Legally, they also had those two weeks, so if I broke the contract, I would have to pay a fine that I could not afford. After two weeks, I flew back to Lithuania during Thanksgiving and the apartment was finally sold. My kids were sad I wasn't with them for the holiday. We always have a nice family dinner on Thanksgiving, but they understood.

Our Vilnius apartment

The second trip to Lithuania in November was only a few days. My dad didn't ask why I came back again so quickly. He was just happy to see me and assumed it was just another one of those "stop by Lithuania on the way to a business trip" cases. I had done a few of those before, so it seemed no big deal to him. On the day of my departure, I went to see him once again. We sat for a bit, then I kissed my dad and waved goodbye to him. I needed to get to the airport. I told him I loved him and he said back with a smile "Go already!"

On December 31st, my sister and I, along with my childhood friends and a few of my father's friends, gathered at the cemetery to say our final goodbyes.

WHEN DOUBT TOOK OVER

February 2020

This is when I really had to stop and self-reflect. I wasn't sure I was being honest with myself and I wasn't convinced that my life was so awesome. In addition to not recovering from 2019 yet, a few weeks earlier, my mom gave us a scare as well. It all turned out to be okay, but for a few hours, we were

watching my mom at the hospital experiencing what we learned later was going into a pain shock. My sister and I didn't know if she just had a stroke or if there was a tumor of some sort and the doctors were about to tell us how sick she was. I felt the ground going out from under me. After seeing what my dad had just gone through, I could not bear to think that my mom could be gone too. I just couldn't process it. I didn't want to process it and I was so grateful and relieved that it didn't turn out to be anything serious.

What positive outlook could one possibly find in any of what had happened in 2019? Was I delusional? Don't answer that...

Writing about all the positives that happened in 2019 was easier than I thought. The first very obvious thought that came to my mind was that I was very happy at my new job. I started listing all that was good, starting in May.

CHALLENGE ACCEPTED. THROWING PUNCHES BACK BY LISTING ALL GOOD THAT HAPPENED IN 2019

May 2019

While recovering from the surgery in April, I had a lot of time, so I went through phone screenings and phone interviews. I ended up starting a really good job mid-May where I met great people and my career took off once again. Some of my former colleagues have since joined me at the new company and I couldn't imagine a better team or a better job for myself.

83

June, July, and August 2019

I spent every weekend in Cape Cod, walking along the beach every Friday, Saturday, and Sunday. My knee got better and better and by August, I was even able to run a mile!

The new job didn't require travel, so I spent a lot more time with my family. I worked a lot, I learned a lot and at the same time, I had a ton of fun! I got a raise and I no longer worried about the ability to pay for my dad's nursing home, even if the apartment in Lithuania didn't get sold. For the first time in my life, I could actually relax a bit and not worry about finances. My dad lived for eight more months, but in May, we didn't know what would happen.

September 2019

I got an opportunity to go to Chennai, India, for work and arranged my travel so that I could "swing by" Lithuania to visit my father on his birthday. I already had a trip planned for mid-November, but this was another opportunity to see him, especially on his birthday. As it turned out, it was his last birthday.

November 2019

Back in April, a good friend of mine asked if I would visit London with her. Since I knew I had to close on the apartment in Lithuania, we planned the trip around that. I had such a great time with her for three days, visiting museums, sightseeing, and just generally enjoying each other's company. It is very hard to describe how grateful I was for that trip. It is so emotionally draining to visit nursing homes in general, but to see your father decline is close to unbearable. That trip to London gave me the fuel I needed to keep going.

Mid-November was my daughter's 14th birthday and we were planning a big party. She had been preparing for it for the six months prior and she couldn't wait. I landed in Boston on the day of her birthday and we had a big party that weekend. The kids had a ton of fun and I got to see my friends as well. Everyone had a blast.

December 2019

I was back in the US after the second trip to Lithuania in November. The ski season was about to start and everyone was excited to see their winter friends, ski coaches, and to hit the slopes! I took a break from teaching skiing that season. I didn't know if I would be able to ski myself after the surgery, but I put on my custom-made ACL knee brace and headed out. My knee worked just fine!

My sister and I spent a week together in Vilnius, Lithuania. After we left Lithuania in 1992, we never got to go back there at the same time. After my father's funeral, we went back to the hotel to rest. It was December 31st. My friend Dina was kind enough to invite my sister and I to spend New Year's at her house. I love visiting her and her husband when I come to Vilnius but, as one may imagine, we weren't in a very festive mood. However, we decided to go out and walked around Vilnius. It is a truly beautiful city and words can't describe the magic of Vilnius, especially at midnight on December 31st at Cathedral Square in the center of the city. It was magical, between the music and the fireworks and us watching people celebrating the new year in the city that we were both born in so many years ago!

January 2020

My dad was no longer suffering. My kids got to see him and got to know him a little. They know that whenever anyone asked their grandpa how he was, he would always answer, "THE BEST!" and he always meant it!

March 2020

My dear friend was still sick. There is no cure for that beast, BUT there was a surgery, there are drugs to keep it under control and her latest scans were good! I get to talk to her often and she inspires me with her wisdom and positive outlook on life. I love her dearly.

I am surrounded by my amazing family and friends. I continue to meet new people that are interesting and passionate. My kids tell me they love me and even though there is an occasional eye roll followed by, "Mom, stop embarrassing me!" I know they enjoy my company. My husband told me recently (after 24 years together) that marrying me was the best decision he made in his life. I teased him that I just went with the flow, but I am pretty happy I did!

Unfortunately, it has been a vicious cycle and I can continue this chapter with the punches life started throwing again in March, but the reader knows the major ones by now. Overall, I can say that I have been able to throw punches back and find good even in something as horrible as my daughter's journey of cancer treatment. It truly does help to stay calm and cope with the most stressful and most painful punches of all, seeing your child suffer.

Here is what I wrote in my journal in April after the first round of chemo was completed,

"We spent a lot of **quality time** with Elena over the last month. We had many frank conversations and I got to witness her strength and confidence. So many **inspiring moments**. On a few occasions, she said how much she loves to spend time with me and how much she missed me when I traveled for work. I knew she didn't like me traveling and I always explained that if she wanted to keep doing ballroom dancing and ski racing, mommy has to travel. For a glimpse of a second, I felt that guilt that working moms feel...and then I didn't. I told her that perhaps her **high appreciation for our time together** now comes from those times we didn't see each other that much. She called me her **best friend** yesterday. I don't know how often 14-year-olds say that to their mothers, but **I will cherish that moment, along with many hugs and kisses we exchanged this month for as long as I live.**"

THE LONGER LIST OF TRAGEDIES IN YOUR LIBRARY, THE EASIER IT IS TO COUNT YOUR BLESSINGS AND KEEP CALM

The amount of information we can keep in our brains at any given time is fascinating. I might not remember what I came to the kitchen for, having to go back empty-handed, but for some reason, I remember details from my life that I wish I could forget. I debated whether to include this list in the book and if it added any value to the story line. I came to the conclusion that by taking you on this journey, you might better understand why I tend to stay calm, especially in situations that are not life threatening.

- When one of my classmate's was 10, his mother was killed in their home by robbers that took whatever electronics they had. I have a few memories of this boy. In second grade, the teacher put him in front of the whole class and wrote out on the board all the classes in which he got a D. It was all of them. He stood there with tears coming down his face. Learning disabilities weren't diagnosed at this time. Social workers didn't exist. Sometimes I wonder if anyone really gave a damn about what was going on in kids' lives. It seems like humiliation was a technique of some sort to motivate learning. Perhaps it is just my perception.

- When I was 12 or so, our neighbor got killed by his "buddies" while we were supposedly home and should have heard something. It was a brutal death. He was tortured. Nobody knew the motive and the killers were never found. He was in his mid-20s, had a wife and a small kid. All the neighborhood kids loved him, including my sister and me. He would often spend time with us – playing volleyball and just hanging out.

- When I was 16, a classmate in Brookline Highschool drowned in the pool while vacationing with her family on the Cape. We weren't super close friends but just one week prior, we ran into each other and chatted for a bit. It was surreal to think that she was gone. I was at the funeral. I still remember her mother's tears and grief.

- When I was 18, my friend's parents, along with many of their friends, died in a car crash while on a reunion trip in Vegas. While at the funeral, I remember thinking how in the world will my friend and her brother cope losing both parents like this. I thought of my mom and dad and my family situation. I remember thinking that even if my dad doesn't come to reunite with us (for some reason, I was still holding on to the possibility at that point), then at least I still have him. I can call or visit him.

- In my early 20s, my very close friend Tania, who I met in college a couple of years prior and got very close to, drowned while scuba diving in Key West. This one hit me extra hard. I remember sitting in my cube with that same knot in my stomach that I described in the first chapter. When a co-worker stopped by and asked me if I was okay, I couldn't talk. I pointed at an article on my monitor. I stared at it for the last hour. The article said that they called off the search. I told my boss I wasn't feeling well and drove to RI to my friend Olga's house. I needed to be with someone who was going through the same pain. Anna, Olga, Masha, Tania and I all met in the in the first few weeks of entering Northeastern University and spent a ton of time together all throughout college. We were very close. We shared a lot of happy moments together, and unfortunately, we ended up sharing one of the most painful moments of our lives together as well. Being together eased the pain, but it was painful beyond what words can describe.

Tania, Masha, Luba, Anya and Olga

- In my mid-20s, a co-worker's healthy baby stopped breathing six days after birth. The email of the baby's death came only a day or so after the birth announcement. That small, white casket is an image I will never be able to erase.

The list goes on...mothers of friends losing the fight with cancer, father of a very close friend dying from a stroke, my classmate from Brookline High dying of a heart attack a few years ago before reaching his 40s, my friend's brother dying of a heart attack in less than 30 minutes, leaving a wife and a very young daughter behind. He was my age.

I often wonder if my dad, regardless of being so sick, was able to count his blessings. After all, he did have kids he loved. He loved the fact that we were all doing well. He had nine grandkids. It is extremely sad that he only ever got to hug three out of nine, but still.

Maybe he knew that he could have been gone a long time ago and he would never see us grow up and do well in life. Maybe for him, those short moments of joy when he heard our voices over the phone was enough to think he had a life worth living? Maybe he was simply counting his blessings and that was the reason why, when asked how he was, he always answered, "THE BEST!"

I wish every reader to have their libraries be empty of tragedies. In reality though, punches of life are inevitable. You may experience them early in life or later on, but there is no escaping. Being able to focus on the NOW, taking it day by day and finding ways to cope is essential. Looking actively for the good, even if it doesn't come naturally to you, is something worth trying. Finding someone to talk to who could help you search for the good may work as well.

I won't claim that counting your blessings directly correlates to a *Life Worth Living*, but it sure helps to keep my sanity intact, which is essential for my well-being! I have no doubt that for me, having a clear and healthy mind contributes to my happiness and to my ability to cope when a painful punch or two comes my way. It also contributes to the desire and ability to find that purpose in life, which directly contributes to my life being a *Life Worth Living*!

CHAPTER 5

Feeding and Spreading Kindness

"One evening, an old Cherokee told his grandson
about a battle that goes on inside people.

He said, "My son, the battle is between
two 'wolves' inside us all.

One is Evil.
It is anger, envy, jealousy, sorrow, regret, greed,
arrogance, self-pity, guilt, resentment, inferiority, lies,
false pride, superiority, and ego.

The other is Good.
It is joy, peace, love, hope, serenity, humility, kindness,
benevolence, empathy, generosity, truth, compassion and faith."

**The grandson thought about it for a minute
and then asked his grandfather:
"Which wolf wins?"**

**The old Cherokee simply replied,
"The one you feed."**

—CHEROKEE METAPHOR

The stories I have shared so far in this book could be categorized as difficult moments, accidents, sickness and pure evil. When it comes to accidents, I am sure people left behind ask themselves questions such as, "Why did it have to happen?" or "What could I have done to prevent it?" When it comes to strokes or in the case of my daughter's cancer, I continue to question myself, "What could I have done differently?" It is not so much blaming myself, but trying to understand what could have caused it and what I could do in the future to prevent it.

Healthy eating habits are not up for debate in our household but it is always a struggle to find that balance. Chapter three of this book was all about not blaming others but not blaming yourself is worth mentioning as well. We do it often. Well, most people that I know do it often. With that said, I wonder what goes through the mind of people who should blame themselves but instead, they murder and have no regrets. It is that pure evil that I mentioned earlier. When we see pure evil happening in front of us, we feel helpless. Albert Einstein, in one of his many wise quotes challenges us by saying, "The world will not be destroyed by those who do evil, but by those who watch them without doing anything." What can we do? In this chapter, I share moments where I felt completely helpless and stories where I was in a position to feed kindness. I share stories of small acts of kindness that had been shown to me and encourage people to feed and spread kindness. It is something that we can all do and it is something that can truly make a difference in the world, hopefully reducing evil and leading more people to a *Life Worth Living*!

WHEN YOU THINK YOU HAVE SEEN THE WORST AND THINK "NEVER AGAIN"...

I was at work on September 11th, 2001 when we first heard there was an airplane accident in New York City. Along with a few co-workers, we rushed downstairs to a gym that had many TVs. Within minutes, we watched LIVE the second airplane hit the second tower. It became obvious very quickly that it was not an accident. I remember my thoughts racing in all different directions. I knew my immediate family was safe and I didn't know many people in New York. My close friend Anna, though, worked on the 31st top floor at State Street in the Financial District in Boston. I remember thinking since it is a terrorist attack and they are going for towers, who knows what they might hit next. We had no cell phones, but there was a phone hanging on the wall at the gym and so without leaving the sight of the TV, I called her. They were all watching as well.

By 9:30 am, they were all told to go home. You can ask every person who was an adult on September 11th, 2001 and they will remember that day as if it was yesterday. To say I was shaken up is an understatement. There are images that haunt me to this day. The feeling of being helpless, watching people jump to their death as the horror unfolds and not being able to do a thing is not possible to describe. The level of cruelty of the people responsible for the attack is not possible to comprehend either. The only explanation is that they were fed evil from early on.

We said "NEVER AGAIN" in the context of the Holocaust. We said "NEVER AGAIN" in the context of 9/11 but it happened again and again. We do say "NEVER FORGET" and that one is more manageable, but I am not sure how much of a difference it is making. Cruelty continues to happen.

WATCHING WITH MY GRANDMOTHER ANOTHER HORROR UNFOLD

September first is a happy day in Lithuania (all of the former USSR). Every kid starts school on that day. Everyone carries flowers for the teachers. Most kids have huge smiles on their faces, anticipating seeing friends and starting a new chapter, whether it is the first day of the first grade or just the next grade up from the previous year. We wore a very sad looking brown dress for a uniform but on that day, and a few more holidays during the year, we wore this white apron on top of the dress to look more festive (I know, I know, it sounds ridiculous). We looked cute and I have a couple of pictures to prove it! There were parades, there were inspirational speeches all around the school and on TV, there was music, house parties and of course, photos!

Luba's mom Sofiya, 1954

Pictures of a few of Luba's friends on Sept 1st. From left to right, Anna Ortiz, Aliona Tchumanov and Anna Simakoff, mid 80s

Relative Masha. Also Sept 1st but over a decade later. 1998. Dress code is slightly different but the white bow is still a big deal!

September 1st, 2004 was different. It was devastating. It is known as the "Beslan school siege." Chechen terrorists took 1,100 people hostage, including 777 children. Little children. For many, it was the very first day of school, something they looked forward to and it would end up being one of their last days to be alive. They were all kept at the gym. They weren't given food or water. When they were finally freed, they showed people running out in their underwear. Men were carrying kids out. My grandmother and I were glued to the TV for days. I described my grandmother Tonia earlier in this book as someone who didn't usually show emotion. She did not cry when her mother passed away. She didn't cry when we said goodbye and left for the US. She didn't cry on her death bed. But, I saw her brush away tears when they announced at least 200 people (final toll was 333) had died and again later that week when they showed many caskets, including short ones, laid out, and many funerals going on at the same time. Funerals of many seven-year-old children. Unthinkable. Cruel. Evil. Once again, helpless.

AGAIN and AGAIN and AGAIN

The Sandy Hook Elementary School shooting, which occurred on December 14th, 2012, in Newtown, Connecticut brought the memories of the Beslan school siege back. There were so many more shootings since then. It is scary to think, but the Sandy Hook shooting hit me hard. By 2012, I had two daughters, Elena was 7 and Anna was 5. Those sweet faces of the kids that got killed and the parents that were speaking up, begging for change, was too close to home. I didn't express much to the outside world and not even my husband knew how much I cried for those poor kids. The tears would just come rolling down when the image of one of their faces popped up in my head. The words of one of the mothers describing how she looked for her daughter's ponytail to show up...and when it didn't. When she described coming home and going to her daughter's bed, the bed where the girl slept just a few hours ago. For months, when I dropped my kids off to school and their ponytails would disappear from my view, I heard that mother's voice and tears would just roll down. This is the reason why I said at the beginning of the book that I myself have not experienced any real tragedy in life.

PONDER: If the world is destroyed by the people who watch others do evil and not do anything, then WHAT IS IT THAT YOU CAN DO?

As we watch first responders, fire fighters, and doctors saving lives, it is easy to see their impact. We might think we are not strong enough or brave enough to make a difference, but we don't have to be. We can do what is within our reach. It is hard to imagine, although I am not ruling it out entirely, that someone who is surrounded by love and care as a child can all of a sudden turn into a monster. When one grows up surrounded by kind people who lead by example and show what giving a damn and being kind looks like, there is a better chance that someone will pass it along at some point in their life. Every bit of kindness matters.

NOT EVERY ACT OF KINDNESS HAS TO BE HEROIC, SIMPLE ACTS FEED KINDNESS AS WELL

July 2019. My daughter, Elena, and I were at the Jimmy Fund Clinic starting her cycle four of chemo. My daughter felt well enough that day and decided to do an arts and crafts project. She picked out this nice shell and markers to color it with. When we were done a few hours later and

96

we were heading out, we noticed a little seven-year-old girl not having a great day. When I say "felt well enough" or "wasn't having a great day" I mean either the kid wasn't nauseous, weak and miserable or the kid was shaking, pale from all the meds, and in pain all over. There is really no rhyme or reason when it comes to the treatment. You will see kids in wheelchairs too weak to walk and you will see kids smiling and doing crafts while watching a cartoon and receiving chemo. You will see kids, not even hooked up to the IV yet, scream at their parents and nurses and you will see kids with amputated legs smiling and having an okay day. In any case, on the way out, my daughter asked me if she could give the shell to this little girl to maybe brighten her day a little. My first response, due to Covid-19 and many people, including me, being paranoid, was, "I am not sure you are allowed." A few seconds later though, I said, "You know what, why don't you go ask her dad if it is okay with him and if it is, offer it to the girl."

My daughter returned with a huge smile on her face. She said the girl's dad was extremely appreciative and the girl absolutely loved the present. It was such a small gesture. It didn't cost anything; it didn't take much time to make and yet it put a smile on someone's face when they didn't feel well. I loved the fact that my daughter saw the opportunity when she could have just walked by. The thought of giving the girl that shell could have not even crossed her mind.

PONDER: How often do we walk by people and don't even pay attention? When I go for a long walk and once in a while stop to rest for a bit, it is interesting to observe how someone walking by will immediately ask if I am okay and others just walk by. Have you ever thought about what your default is? Is it to ask if someone is okay or walk by thinking it is none of your business?

PRESENTS THAT MAKE AN IMPACT

As you may have guessed by now, I didn't have much growing up. Compared to many of my friends though, one might say I had plenty. In general, I am not a materialistic person. I will always choose an experience over a "thing". With that said, there were a few presents over the years that were extra meaningful to me. Yes, it was what was given to me that made an impact at the moment, but it was people showing me they cared that stayed with me over the years.

- Although Manya supplied most of our clothes, I remember there was one winter where I couldn't go play outside because I didn't have winter boots. I was six. We had a snowstorm and I was stuck at home. I remember the front door opening up and my dad bringing in two pairs of winter boots inside. Both pairs were the same size. This is all he could get and even that was a miracle. Now I wonder who gave him a tip on which store had the boots and how long he had to stay in line to get them. The boots were a few sizes too big on me but it didn't matter. I was happy to get the boots and be able to go play in the snow. I wore them for years. I still remember what they looked like. They were off-white with a grey flower on the side.

- When my father got to visit his brother Misha in Israel, he came back with lots of presents. There were many things Misha's wife Rima packed for us, but the two most memorable were a pair of jeans with Mickey Mouse on the right leg and a beautiful dress for my mom. I wore that pair of jeans for many years and it was the only pair of pants I had when I came to the US. The black velvet dress that my mom wore to her 40th birthday was brought to the US as well. When I met my husband in 1996 and we competed in ballroom dancing competitions among colleges, I wore that dress and felt like a million bucks waltzing around the ballroom.

- When I was 12, my sister got a chance to go to Germany for an exchange program. It wasn't that common and the opportunity was only given to those who had room to host. My sister always did very well in school and so it was supposed to be a big reward. She didn't have a great time there at all and the family who hosted her weren't super nice or hospitable, but she sure made my day when she returned from that trip with a big surprise for me. I mean really big. She walked through the front door carrying a large stuffed bear. I was absolutely speechless when she gave it to me. It was bright yellow and almost my height. Toys like that didn't exist when I was growing up. It was even more special when she later told us she spent all the money she had left on that bear. She could have bought many things for herself, but she chose to spend it on me. We had to leave that bear behind when we left Vilnius and I don't know who ended up being the lucky kid to get it, but a small stuffed monkey, which she also brought for me from that trip, is still in my possession. There was no way I would leave that cutie behind.

- When we came to the US, Manya made sure that a few boxes of clothes waited for us upon our arrival. There was plenty to wear, except I found myself once again without waterproof boots. I can't remember now why I didn't say anything to my mom or my sister but instead chose to walk to school in whatever shoes I had and ignored my wet feet. One day, my friend Irina's mom Rita gave me a pair of black shiny boots. It was the same pair she bought for her own daughter. They cost $20 but she refused to take the money from me. Frankly, I didn't have $20 to give to her so I was glad she refused. I am sure she knew. The funny thing is, she doesn't remember it. I, on the other hand, remember it as if it was yesterday. That act of kindness is hard to forget, especially if you remember how warm and dry your feet were.

- I worked in a tuxedo shop on the corner of Route 9 and Cypress St in Brookline when I started my freshman year at Northeastern University. I lived in a dorm, had a food card, and could manage just fine on my part-time salary. Until of course, I had to buy school books. I don't know now why the scholarship and financial aid didn't take into consideration that significant expense, but I remember not having enough money to buy a $100 C++ textbook. It was our one-year anniversary, mid-September of 1997 when my now husband surprised me with the C++ book after spending about 12 hours helping me study this fascinating subject that took me a very long time to absorb. It may have not been the most romantic anniversary present, but it was one that put a big smile on my face. It has been collecting dust for many years now but it doesn't matter. I will always remember that act of kindness, especially since $100 for my husband at that time was a very significant sum. He was a student himself.

- When I was in my early 20s, I was obsessed with the Harry Potter books. There were only four books out at that time and the fifth one was about to be released. I had a co-worker, Matt, who was one of the nicest people I have met to date. One day, I came to work and found the fifth book of Harry Potter that I so badly wanted that just got released on my desk. He happened to be shopping the night before and decided to surprise me with it. He didn't have to, but I remember how happy he looked that he managed to surprise me with something I didn't expect. When was the last time you managed to get something for someone and totally nailed it? It feels great, doesn't it?

THE RED SUIT THAT MADE AN IMPACT ON HUNDREDS OF PEOPLE

There was one other present. This particular one made an impact not only on my life, but the life of my children, and many people who came to Loon Mountain to take ski lessons over the last 17 years. I wasn't a very athletic kid growing up. I liked to dance, but it wasn't anything competitive or too physically strenuous. It was more for the pleasure of the soul and mind. When I met my husband in 1996 and he attempted to give me a ski lesson in early 1997, that didn't go very well. After falling countless times, I swore I would never do it again. In 1999, however, my husband gave me the most beautiful, one-piece, red ski suit for my 21st birthday along with a ski lesson from a professional. I think it was his last attempt to get me to ski, knowing that if we ended up getting married and having kids, it was the only way to have a skiing family. He was pretty convinced that if the future mom didn't ski, the future kids wouldn't ski much either. I did ask him if I could just wear the beautiful suit and not ski, but that didn't fly. I took that ski lesson and even if my ski technique wasn't that great, I looked absolutely fabulous in that red ski suit! I also fell in love with skiing. A few bruises here and there didn't bother me and I also learned that when you take ski lessons, you might not even fall. It is possible to learn skiing by taking it slow and safe.

Beautiful red snowsuit which led Luba to her skiing career!

For five years, my husband and I took lessons and were a part of the Adult Seasonal Group at Loon Mountain. For 40 days in the winter, we skied with a ski instructor and a group of adults who, like us, wanted to have fun skiing and continuously improve their technique. Continuous improvement is something that I could always see in both skiing and professional life. No matter how good you are at something, there is always something to improve. After five years, we felt it was time to give back to society and start teaching. I loved it so much. Regardless of how hard it was physically at times, especially during school vacations when you taught for six hours a day, ten days straight, I came back to teach skiing year after year.

CHOOSING KINDNESS

In 2019, on the last day of my teaching commitment for the year, while teaching a very adorable seven-year-old girl, I got into a minor ski accident. After a few hours of practicing on the bunny hill turning and stopping, I took four kids up on the Kissing Cousins chair lift. It is a very small chair lift that takes you to a pretty flat and not very long ski trail. We all came down nice and slow. I was leading the kids, keeping a safe distance following my wide turns. It was the most beautiful sunny day and surprisingly, not many people on the trail. At the very bottom, one of the four kids, the seven-year-old girl, came from behind me and crossed the trail in front of me unexpectedly. Both of my skis went on top of hers, causing both of my skis to slowly move to opposite sides, tearing my ACL on my left knee in a very slow motion.

Let's pause here for a second.

> **PONDER:** Put yourself in my shoes (or my ski boots) and think about what would cross your mind at that moment? What do you think you would have said or done? What were different ways one could have reacted?

My first thought was that I wanted to make sure the little girl wasn't scared and wasn't scarred for life after this ski lesson. Since the kids heard me scream from pain, though only for about five seconds, I wanted to make sure they were not traumatized. I hugged her (while waiting for ski patrol) and told her I was perfectly okay. They were to finish the lesson with a different ski instructor. I also went to visit the kids during their lunch break, after ski patrol was done with me and supplied me with a knee brace and crutches. I wanted to see the kids and ask how the rest of their lesson went. As I expected, the accident did make an impact on them. They circled me and asked me how I was feeling. That little adorable seven-year-old had no idea that I would have a long journey to recovery and potentially retire altogether from teaching skiing, but I could tell she felt bad. I had to reassure her I would be as good as new in a few weeks and in the meantime, my kids would have to take care of me so I would get to relax. We hugged it out again and all the kids left with a smile.

When you have to make a choice, choose to think about how your actions might impact someone else. What is the desired outcome? When given the choice, choose kindness. It does make a difference and not only for the people on the receiving end of your kindness. When you express compassion and gratitude (more about that in the next chapter), it affects your brain and your level of happiness as well. As mentioned, multiple times now throughout the book, but I will continue to repeat it, at the end of the day, the gratitude, compassion, kindness and happiness all lead to a *Life Worth Living*!

Loon Mountain, Lincoln NH

CHAPTER 6

Being Grateful

"The most important quality to have toward your day is gratitude for what you have experienced, even for what was hard and what allowed you to learn and grow."

-DALAI LAMA XIV, THE BOOK OF JOY: LASTING HAPPINESS IN A CHANGING WORLD

This chapter is about connecting with people and being grateful for having them in your life. I am talking about those deep connections that are based on trust, empathy, respect, and knowing that you have people who will have your back when you need it. It is about you being that person who will be there for your friends, family, co-workers, and strangers who might have no one else to turn to at the lowest points of their lives.

Introductions:

Vesta: We met in the first grade.

Jasha: We met when we were teenagers, only a couple of years before I left for the United States.

Victorija and Dina: My Vilnius classmates, grades one to eight.

Aliona Tchumanov: Classmate from grades five to eight and one of my closest friends to this day.

Vika: I met Vika through Jasha when we were already in our 20s.

Irina and Ilona: Two of my closest friends that I met when I arrived in the US. I owe it to my sister for introducing me to these incredible women (teenagers then).

Rita: I met Rita at Brookline High School.

Masha, Olga M., Anna Ortiz: I met these ladies at Northeastern University, freshman year in 1996.

SHOWING UP WHEN NO ONE EXPECTING

Vesta and I met in the first grade. She was a straight-A student, always on top of her game and she lived near me so we would always meet at a bus stop and go to school together. I don't remember what exactly we had in common back then besides living nearby, but nevertheless, we spent a lot of time together. The one thing I remember we did have in common was the fact that we both liked to come to school earlier and not be late. I still don't like being late. You will see me at the airport always way ahead of time, not risking it. I never liked the adrenaline of wondering if I would make it or not.

Fast forward a few decades.

Vesta didn't have to visit my father and grandmother on New Year's. She didn't have to go to the hospital and talk to the doctors when my grandmother first got admitted in April of 2017. She didn't have to drive me around town in search of a wheelchair for my father so he could attend my grandmother's funeral. She didn't have to visit my dad at the nursing home countless times when he was alone. She brought so much joy to my dad when she visited him with her kids. He remembered her younger daughter's sweet hugs and later told me about that visit with a smile. She didn't have to do any of it, and I only listed a handful of things she has done over the years. She did them though because she gave a damn. She showed up.

**Vesta with Tonia,
in the Uzhupio
kitchen, mid 90s**

Luba with Vesta, mid 90s

HAVING SOMEONE BY YOUR SIDE AT YOUR LOWEST POINT

I could easily write a book just describing the impact Jasha made on my life and my family in Vilnius. Jasha and I, along with our friends Marta and Aliona, were inseparable in the early 90s. Those couple of years before I left Vilnius were the most memorable years of my childhood.

My children now are the same age as I was back then and, boy, do they have a different life! When we were kids, we were free as birds, roaming around the town of Vilnius doing absolutely nothing except having a blast talking and laughing. It was doing nothing, the talking and laughing that created that bond for life.

Luba with Jasha, 1991

Luba with her husband (he visited Vilnius once!) and friend Jasha

Aliona and Jasha seeing me off at the Airport in the late 90s

Each time I see Jasha in Vilnius, it is like we just hung out yesterday. We pick up exactly where we left off. Regardless of the circumstances, whether he is driving me around, arranging a funeral for my grandmother, pushing me to find the courage and strength to do what needs to get done when I have no more strength left, or just listening to my outrage because of bureaucracy and the annoying paperwork, we always manage to still laugh and find joy in our conversations.

WHAT GOT ME THROUGH 1992

Luba's Wall. 1992

It was time for me to leave Lithuania. I was scared and sad to leave my dad, grandmother and friends behind. We were at the train station, ready to hop on an overnight train to Moscow to catch a plane to JFK and then Boston. My friends came to say goodbye and see me off. They each took some currency of the paper money (rubles at that time) and signed them. My friend Jasha signed a special poster for me.

In Boston, my sister, mom and I, along with uncle and grandma all lived in a two-bedroom apartment. My sister and I slept in the open living room that had no door. We had no school desks or any space of our own. I was allowed to use a wall in the hallway to put up my sacred possessions that reminded me of my friends I left behind in Lithuania.

I still have a box with letters from Vesta, Marta, Aliona, and Jasha from when I just came to the US. The letters, the posters and signed rubles made me feel close to home. Looking at the wall and going through letters would bring me closer to them, especially at the moments when all I wanted to do was to cry and get on the next available flight back to Vilnius.

That, along with the two friends I met in Boston in 1992, Irina and Ilona, was what helped get through those difficult teenage years upon arriving in the US at the age of 14. Irina (Irka to me) and Ilona both live in different states now. I see them once a year at most, but they are a significant part of my life and I can't imagine my life without their friendship.

Luba with her two closest friends, Irina and Ilona, mid 90s

Luba with Ilona   **Luba with Irina, 2005**

GOING ABOVE AND BEYOND AND NOT EVEN KNOWING IT

I met Rita at Brookline High School. Rita was among a group of Russian-speaking kids who all came to the US at the same time as me. We took dance classes together, spent a lot of time hanging out after school when time permitted, and stayed in touch over the years. I was so lost in 2019 with all the paperwork I had to obtain to deal with real estate affairs in Vilnius, I didn't know where to turn. Not only was it complicated figuring out what I needed to do while in Vilnius, I needed documents from my mom to allow me to do whatever I needed to do on her behalf there. It wasn't only Rita's expertise as a lawyer that I am grateful for. It is her friendship and support. After the knee surgery when I was seriously at my lowest and had just started a new, exciting but demanding job, having to go back to Vilnius, Rita came to the rescue. Not only did she draft whatever documents I needed, but she also drove to my mom to get her signature, drove to the center of Boston to get the right apostille, and FedExed the documents to me right in time for yet another trip to Vilnius. It may have seemed like no big deal to her, but it meant more than the world to me at that particular moment. My ability to keep my dad in a high-end nursing home and get the best possible care depended on that piece of paper. It was priceless.

HAVING SUPPORT WHEN IT HITS YOU HARD

Northeastern University, freshman year in 1996 would turn out to be a very significant year for me. Not only did I meet my now husband within the two weeks of arrival on campus, but I also met my now friends for over 20 years. I grew up with these amazing ladies by my side. We have seen each other get married and have children. They were there for me a week after I gave birth to my older daughter. That day, when they came to find me exhausted, unable to even walk downstairs to the kitchen, they sprang into action. Olga took care of the baby and sent me off to shower, for which I was so grateful! Anna went food shopping while Masha cleaned the kitchen and cooked. I remember what she brought me upstairs as one of the best meals of my life, fried potatoes with hotdogs. Not my current choice of food but that plate of deliciousness will always stay in my memory.

We have watched our children become teenagers. We have seen what pain a divorce can bring and how the pain from that subsides over the years. We were there during happy times and some of the worst times of our lives. There is some pain, such as the pain of losing my grandmother and father, that I could truly share only with my friends in Vilnius. There is the other kind of pain, the pain of losing a friend, which I mentioned in the previous chapter, that I can only truly share with Masha, Olga, and Anna.

**Luba with friends Masha, Olga and Anna
Celebrating Masha's birhtday! Boston 2015**

REALIZING YOU HAVE A LOT MORE IN COMMON

I met Vika through Jasha when we were already in our 20s. She will agree with me that we were extremely different people. We laughed a couple of years ago when I shared with her that I just learned what "Louis Vuitton" was. Yup, I was 40 when I was introduced to that expensive brand while walking around Boston Copley Store with a few of my colleagues who came out of state and wanted to shop around. Since 2017, I stayed with Vika whenever I came to Vilnius. During some of my visits, when Jasha was out of state on business, she would take over and be the one to come with me to different offices and in many cases, translate Lithuanian documents, schedule appointments with notaries, real estate agents and whatever else I needed to get done in Vilnius. We would stay up late, enjoy some wine, and talk about life. Her openness and her willingness to ask for career-related or personal development advice is admirable. Over the years, I realized how much more in common we have. Most importantly though, we care about each other and we will always be there for each other.

Luba with daughter Anna and friend Vika
Sunday brunch during the Vilnius visit in April 2018

IT DOESN'T HAVE TO BE FIREWORKS

We don't have to do anything major to make an impact. Sometimes, it is grabbing a cup of coffee or a quick call that makes a difference. Each time I visited Vilnius over the years, but especially in the last three years, those visits were very difficult emotionally. My friend Victorija, with whom I went to elementary and middle school in Vilnius, would often meet me for a quick lunch, coffee, or just a lovely chat. She visited me in Boston years ago and it was awesome to introduce her to my Boston friends. It was one of those few rare moments when I got to blend my two worlds. She gave a guided tour of Vilnius to both of my kids when they came to visit and it meant a lot. The pictures we now have from those tours are priceless memories.

Each time my friend Dina (also a classmate from childhood) invited me over to her house for dinner, it was time away from the reality of watching my father decline. It took my mind off what was to come soon and it helped me keep my sanity more than she and her husband probably realized at the time. When she invited my sister and I to spend the 2020 New Year's with her family, she wasn't thinking that the two sisters who just buried their father wouldn't be that much fun to be around. It was selfless. She invited us to make sure we had a place to go to and enjoy the evening as much as one could after a funeral, let alone your father's funeral. Even though we politely declined the invitation, my sister and I were extremely grateful.

BEING GRATEFUL MORE THAN EVER DURING COVID-19

This global madness caused by the pandemic affected millions of people and it will make history. I am sure our grandchildren will be learning about it in schools. Nobody could have predicted back in March that by June (when I am writing this), there would still be no light at the end of the tunnel. I hear from friends things are getting a bit better in Lithuania, daycares are opening up and people are back to the offices at full capacity, but here in Boston and many other states in the US, not much has changed. In many areas, after restrictions loosened up a bit, the number of cases has gone up significantly again. We can argue until we are blue in the face that it is because more people are getting tested or the media is out to scare us, but the fact stays the same, nobody is going anywhere any time soon.

Having an immunocompromised child added a bit more to the scare. Having a couple of friends who live very close to us taking care of ALL the food shopping so we didn't have to go to stores was helpful beyond words. There is this expression in Russian which is "**Не имей сто рублей, а имей сто друзей.**" The meaning is similar to, "A friend in court is better than a penny in purse" and word for word translation is, "It is better to have a hundred friends than a hundred rubles." You start to truly understand what it means when there are no available grocery delivery times, CVS is out of hair clippers and your kid needs/wants one NOW because chemo kicked in, causing hair to fall out. You really appreciate people willing to help in any way they can when your child started making cinnamon rolls to surprise you but we are out of flour. As my friend's mother (while giving me the flour) and many others this month said, "**IT TAKES A VILLAGE!**"

While I was open about my daughter's diagnosis and had a private Facebook group to keep friends, relatives and a few co-workers updated, I didn't share more widely until almost the end of the treatment. I shared on Facebook, as part of an inspirational message, that we were heading out soon to the Jimmy Fund Clinic to start cycle six of chemo. So many people showed their support, it was overwhelming. All I meant to do with that message was to share that I chose to be happy, to show that I could either cry about the fact that chemo was starting again or be happy and think of it as one day closer to being healthy! To my surprise, people that I hadn't spoken to for years reached out to let me know they were there for me and my family. It was special beyond words.

I am extremely grateful to be surrounded by family, close friends, and in general, people who simply give a damn. It is a true blessing.

::: PONDER
PONDER: Who are those special people in your life? When was the last time you reached out to them to see how they are doing? Do they know that if they ever face a challenging situation, you will be there for them?
:::

WHEN COMPLETE STRANGERS GO ABOVE AND BEYOND - MY HUSBAND'S STORY

We have these unspoken expectations from close relatives and friends to come to the rescue when something happens. It might be a given in some families and some might take it for granted but overall, we say thank you, accept the help, and move on. When a stranger chooses to help, the level of gratitude jumps higher. My husband and I have had many conversations about our families and what brought both of us to the US, but it wasn't until I started working on this book that he shared the depth of his story. I talk a lot in this book about counting your blessings, different perspectives, and being grateful. Well, his story of coming to the US shows just how important it is to give a damn and help whenever possible, even if it is a stranger who needs help.

My husband talks about the changes that Mikhail Gorbachev, former leader of the Soviet Union, brought to the Soviet Union and the world. He talks about how the reforms led to the complete collapse of the economy. He talks about how everything people were aiming for lost its value.

It is important to describe in detail exactly what took place prior to his departure and what it took him to get to that point to understand the magnitude of the stranger's help who happened to be standing nearby. The full story told by my husband is below. In summary, after a lot of stressful moments leading to the departure itself and with border control back in St. Petersburg, once he was finally on the plane to Helsinki, he thought to himself, *"No one can stop me now or hold me up for any reason. I am going to the world where law rules and if you don't do anything wrong, you have nothing to be afraid of."*

116

Not so fast. He had another couple of flights before getting to Boston and prior to boarding the next flight, from Helsinki to Miami, another challenge awaited. After a mistake was made with his US visa, instead of acknowledging it, the airline employee at the gate decided to play it safe and not let my husband board the flight to the US. Instead, she handed him a boarding pass to go back to St. Petersburg, the place where he had just left a few hours back. He was trying to make sense of what was happening, watching his luggage being taken off the airplane which was going from Helsinki to Miami. There was so much commotion, it started to draw people's attention. Thankfully, one of the people standing behind my husband in line happened to be the Chief Deputy of the American Embassy in Helsinki. He was the one who asked to see my husband's passport, looked at the visa, discovered that there was a simple typo in the visa, made a quick call, and straightened everything out.

Here is the full story my husband tells,

Most people in the West know the changes that Mikhail Gorbachev brought to the Soviet Union and the world—the end of the Cold War, the fall of Berlin Wall and the reforms collectively known as Perestroika. That's why he probably received the Nobel Peace Prize. Not many in the West know, however, the effect these reforms had on the people in a country which takes up 1/5 of the globe. The reforms led to the complete collapse of the economy, many people lost their jobs, others weren't getting paid, and those who were getting paid couldn't afford to buy anything. Of course, no one was starving, you had the basics at the stores, but there were lines for everyday items like milk, bread, or sugar. The inflation was so high that those who had any savings lost everything. The economic difficulties were staggering, but that was minor compared to other changes Gorbachev probably unwillingly brought in. The seeds of the new market economy got into "the soil" cultivated for over 70 years of communism. Those times resembled something between the Wild West and New York during the era of Prohibition. The country was quickly turning from being an "Evil Empire" to becoming an "Evil Banana Republic." At that time, we did not see any hope for the future of fundamental research, investment in science, education, or technology. We found ourselves in between the two epochs, everything we were aiming for lost value and the new values were not attractive to me at all. However, due to the reforms, the Iron Curtain fell and the borders were opened—you could go to another country and do what you loved there. Unfortunately, no one wanted us now, we were not a refugee of the authoritarian regime anymore.

I decided to go to the United States and look for a job there. As I did not have relatives, the only legal way was to get admitted to a graduate school. You could study for an advanced degree, have tuition reimbursed, and receive a small stipend. In return, however, you had to do research for the professor who sponsored your admission. I decided to go for it in the spring of 1991. English was a big obstacle. My level of English was the ability to read "Russian to English dictionary" at best, forget about taking TOEFL and GRE. It took almost two years to get my English to the level where I could prepare and take the exams. There was no Internet, no native speakers to practice with, no movies or podcasts in English. Even the preparation guides for the exams were available only in one library and none of the materials could be checked out or copied. I visited that library every single day as if it were my job for almost a year. This was the hardest task I ever accomplished in my life and it was the hardest time of my life. I was finishing up a PhD dissertation, worked part-time, and studied English on top of it all. I took the entrance exams and got a decent score, however, my resumes and letters were left unanswered. Over those two years, I sent hundreds of resumes to different universities and got no answers. The most I ever got was a standard reply postcard. I started to lose hope, often thinking that all these efforts were useless. The only person that ever replied to me was Professor Tatyana Roziner from BU—an amazing person. She wrote me a long letter with tons of recommendations and advised me to keep trying. The most amazing thing about the letter was that it was handwritten. She put a lot of effort in for a stranger and I was very grateful.

Finally, in January of 1994, I got an acceptance letter to the PhD Program from one of the universities in Boston. Can you imagine my level of joy?

It is like an athlete training very hard for many years having no hope, but finally being admitted to the National Olympic team.

As if getting to the point of departure from Russia wasn't challenging enough, departure itself brings back bad memories. For the trip to even happen, I needed money for the plane ticket and to survive financially the first month in the States. Two thousand dollars does not sound like a lot, but back then, it was a big sum and I had to borrow from all my friends. When the time came to quit my job and tell everyone, it was not received well. No one felt indifferent. Many did not approve, even considered this a betrayal, others envied me, and a few friends felt sympathetic.

Even though I didn't have everyone's support, I was ready to leave the country anyway. I was finally at the airport. I said goodbye to my parents and friends and headed toward the passport control. To this day, going through passport control always gives me a feeling of horror even many years later... There are many reasons why that booth could cause anxiety. Life in the USSR, despite the common belief, was quite free. We did not have many things to be afraid of or to be cautious about. No parking tickets, no fines for unpaid utilities, nor unexpected bills for "free" subscriptions, no eviction for an unpaid mortgage, etc. The only thing I was afraid of was the government bureaucracy machine. Usually, it existed somewhere in a parallel universe and if you did not do anything stupid, you weren't affected by it. But, if you passed nearby, its huge cogwheel could grab you and drag you in, seriously messing up your plans or even your life.

Going through border patrol is one of those experiences when you never know what may happen. In that instance, I gave my passport to the security officer. For whatever reason, those officers are mostly angry women with no smile on their faces. After a few questions, she told me to wait, took my passport, and left. Ten minutes later, I started to get nervous. My flight was about to depart. I waited for a half an hour, thinking about everything they could possibly hold me for and not let me go. Finally, she came back and gave me my passport. I ran to the departure gate. I had a connection in Helsinki and was flying to the States from there. I clearly remember thinking once I got on that plane, no one can stop me now or hold me up for any reason. I am going to the world where law rules and if you don't do anything wrong you have nothing to be afraid of.

While in Helsinki, half an hour before departure, I heard my name. Over the intercom, they asked me to come to the departure gate. As soon as I approached the counter, the airline employee told me:

"Sir, you are not eligible to come to the United States. We booked your flight back to Saint Petersburg. It departs in an hour. Here is your boarding pass."

While she was speaking, I observed through the glass wall behind the counter my luggage being unloaded from the plane. My stress level exceeded ten points on the Richter scale. I was losing everything I had worked for in the last four years and did not want to give up so easily.

"Excuse me, can you please explain what is going on?" I asked the employee.

She replied, "We just got a fax from the American Consulate in Saint Petersburg stating that you are not eligible to enter the US."

"Can I please see the fax?" I asked.

What the FAX is going on? I thought to myself. I did not sell drugs to prostitutes, nor was I ever a member of any radical party...

"You will not be able to understand it, it is in Finnish," the airline employee replied.

"How come the fax from the American Consulate in Russia is written in Finnish?" I pushed.

It was clearly going nowhere and started to draw the attention of people behind me in line. The conversation was interrupted by a gentleman who was right behind me in line. The Finnair lady's face changed immediately. I did not understand them as they spoke Finnish, but it was clear that the guy was a big boss. Then, he turned to me and asked for my passport, checked the visa, and called somewhere. A few minutes later, I got my passport back with the boarding pass to my US flight. I was boiling inside and my face, the color of a bright red tomato, clearly showed it as well. I was speechless and puzzled. What just happened?

It turned out that my savior was the Diplomatic mission Chief Deputy of the American Embassy in Helsinki! He came to see off his mother who had a ticket on the same flight. The fax did not exist. There was a typo in my visa. Back then, the visa was just a stamp in the passport with dates written by hand.

Finnair decided not to take a chance just in case I was not admitted to the US and they would be responsible to fly me back. It was safer and cheaper for them to turn me back in Helsinki.

The level of gratitude I experienced when I finally got on the flight to the US toward that man is beyond any words. To this day, I am grateful for the fact that this man, who could easily just not interfere, chose to interfere and help.

THE HAPPY CHAIN OF EVENTS

I don't want to imagine what could have become of my husband's life had he been forced to return to St. Petersburg that day. People do make mistakes, I understand. It was a human error that another human chose not to deal with because it was a bit of extra effort. They couldn't imagine the impact it could have made on someone's life. They didn't stop to think how hard the journey was for my husband to get to that point. We will never know what made the airline employee decide that the solution to the visa problem was to get my husband on the next flight back to St. Petersburg. It was not the right solution. I am grateful that the Chief Deputy of the American Embassy in Helsinki happened to be standing behind my husband in line. I am grateful he chose to help and I am grateful that my husband made it to the US.

I am also extremely grateful that my husband had enough courage back in 1996 to ask me to dance with him. I am grateful to a friend who, knowing how much I loved to dance, told me there was a ballroom dance club gathering on the second floor of the Northeastern University Cafeteria. I am grateful that I made the decision to go check it out and chose to accept my husband's invitation to try waltzing around that cafeteria. It was a special dance that led us to our family. I am grateful for my family. Family is everything. Family is what makes my life, *The Life Worth Living!*

PART 2

Applying our lived experiences to professional life

What friends and colleagues had to say...

"I remember when I first met Luba and we started talking about the journey that led her to Boston. While I found that journey incredibly interesting, the real lasting impression I had was of her positive and genuine nature.

At some level, I think we all realize that no one else can control your feelings besides you. So, if you want to be more positive, choose to be more positive. We may all realize this simple fact but sometimes life's roller coaster can make it very hard to live this truth.

Luba has figured this part out and has placed positivity at the core of her personality. "

Bob Malone, President
LeapFrog Systems

"From the first day when Luba limped into our initial meeting with a knee brace and a big smile, she has been the definition of an upbeat, positive presence. She has continued her 'can do' approach every day, regardless of the professional or personal challenges that came her way over our last year plus working together—and there have been more than anyone single person should expect. I pride myself on being able to see the world as a half-full glass rather than half empty, but Luba's daily example reminds me that I too can pour a little more into my glass."

Gary Carvalho, Chief Delivery Officer
LeapFrog Systems

"It's hard to believe that I've only known Luba for a little over a year. In that timeframe, she has made such a positive impact on our company's culture that I will be forever grateful for. She has built such strong relationships with her colleagues here and has also arguably been our best recruiter, bringing several former colleagues aboard, largely because they wanted to work with Luba again.

As I write this, in August 2020, we are in the midst of a global pandemic that has surely given plenty of opportunities for people to feel like the world is stacked against them, but not Luba. She is always able to see the positive in any situation she is dealt, and she's willing to help others find positivity as well.

After our company shifted to working remotely, Luba was one of the leaders in creating new avenues of communication, both for work productivity and a social standpoint. This allowed us to feel connected with our colleagues and foster a collaborative and empathetic environment where we can feel comfortable showing vulnerability, knowing it will be received with support, not judgment. My admiration for Luba's outlook on life grows by the day, and I'm honored to call her a colleague, and a friend."

Mike Corson - VP, People & Culture
LeapFrog Systems

"One of the most remarkable experiences I had working with Luba, was witnessing her ability to bring calmness to crowded and noisy rooms. Her calm demeanor, and ability to relate to people quickly and easily allows her to connect with, and relate to people not only deeply, but with lightning speed. In my 20+ year career, I don't think I've ever witnessed anyone build trusting relationships across all levels of an organization as quickly or as strongly as Luba does. In doing so, when you're in the middle of a crisis, and she tells you things are going to be ok, you believe her. Luba has the rare talent of speaking truth to power in ways that instantly remove all the usual antibodies of fear, resentment, and personal risk that typically accompany difficult feedback. She can bring change to the most obstinate managers, while keeping everything safe and fun, and leaving everyone wanting more."

Leigh Heyman

"When I met Luba, I found her to be warm, engaging, and driven. Over time (and the closer we became) I learned that there was so much more to her! Luba has been highly successful navigating and rising through the ranks in the still male-dominated technology industry. She enthusiastically dives into identifying and solving engineering and business obstacles. However, it's not just her technical skills that I have found so impressive. Luba is a fantastic teammate, mentor, confidant, and friend. She understands the art of listening and uses this unique skill to build strong teams, encourage innovative thinking, and challenge people to achieve their goals. Luba is a true thought leader who embodies the characteristics needed in executive roles! I can't wait to see her keynote speech at a large tech conference or on a Ted Talk. In fact – I hope to be sitting in the front row!"

Brooke Satti Charles

CHAPTER 7

Leadership, Feedback and Decision-Making

"The measure of intelligence is the ability to change."
—ALBERT EINSTEIN

What do finding courage, giving a damn, not blaming others, not judging, not pointing out negative personality traits behind someone's back, spreading kindness, counting your blessings, building relationships, being grateful, and seeing different perspectives mean in the professional life? How do all the "ponder" questions in previous chapters help in work-related scenarios?

I will share a few of my work-related experiences over the years. What happens in our personal lives, as well as our work lives, shapes how we act and how we think in both of those worlds. We may act differently depending on the environment, but overall, we are the same people.

The world that is most familiar to me is Information Technology. However, when it comes to leadership, healthy work environment, honest communication, and many other aspects of human behavior, the field that one works in makes no difference. No matter what your professional world is, you will find at least some, if not all, aspects described in this book applicable.

WHY WAS THIS CHAPTER WRITTEN IF IT IS A MEMOIR?

In the beginning of the book, I shared a bit of my journey embracing the Computer Science degree, despite my lack of interest in physics or even basic programming skills. I touched a bit on the importance of communication when a project isn't going according to plan and the importance of finding courage in that context. I have been in the industry for over 20 years and have been in positions such as a support engineer, quality assurance engineer, systems engineer, software engineer, multiple leadership roles, a trainer and a coach.

I can clearly see how our mindset is truly the key to progress and success in whatever it is we want to embrace. When I started this memoir, I had no plans to make it a work-related book. However, I could not help but see the correlation after each chapter was written. The stories from my corporate journey started popping up one after the other and I realized that there was a lot I was still holding on to, blaming and not letting go. It was time to ponder, self-reflect, find some lessons and let go. Thus, this chapter was written.

LEADING WITH COMPASSION

"We desperately need more leaders who are committed to courageous, wholehearted leadership and who are self-aware enough to lead from their hearts, rather than unevolved leaders who lead from hurt and fear"

—BRENEE BROWN

I have worked for many leaders over the years. Some I remember as inspiring, some as overprotective, and some just not giving a damn. In some cases, I worked through the night just to make sure they had all they needed, and then in other cases, I could hardly wait for the clock to strike five pm. In some very rare cases, it was because I was no longer learning and found the job extremely boring but, in most instances, it depended on the boss I had. Everyone wants to have a mentor or at least someone who gives a damn and will have their back.

FINDING COURAGE TO MAKE A TOUGH CHOICE

Introductions:

Me: A mother of two teenage daughters. A professional woman who was a brand-new mom once, having to make that tough choice of going back to work or be a full-time mom.

My sister Ella: A working mother of four and now a business owner.

Joy: One of the best managers I have ever had. Someone who showed me what true servant leadership is before this term was even widely known. She was also the very first person who introduced me as an "Agile Coach". I looked at her briefly thinking "I am?" and this is how my coaching journey began.

Chuba: A high-level executive who surprised me with a small act of kindness.

Luba with her kids, toddler Elena and new born Anna

Regrets aren't really my thing. As far as this chapter goes, I will share a story about me switching from a comfortable job at Company A, where I had earned respect, didn't face new challenges, and had a flexible schedule, to a job at Company B. I switched jobs when I was four months pregnant. The person who interviewed and hired me was a very nice guy and he was the one whom I had to tell I was pregnant. He congratulated me and asked me if I was planning to come back to work after maternity leave. I assured him that I had no intention to stay home after my bundle of joy arrived.

Fast forward a few months, I was back from my maternity leave, excited to come to work. I had a new boss. I won't go into the difficulties of being a new mom and nursing and having to pump milk at work, but I will say it wasn't a walk in the park and the new boss didn't make it any easier.

On my second day back, I got a call from my nanny. My 11-week old baby was screaming on the other end. She refused to take the bottle I had left.

It was 4:45 pm. As I was walking towards my cubicle the next morning at 8:45 am, I noticed my boss standing next to it. He waited until I got closer, looked at his watch, shook his head in disapproval, and went to his office. He called me in later that day to tell me that I should either stay home and raise my baby or I should make arrangements. I didn't know much about emotional intelligence back then and I wasn't a Professional Coach but somehow, even though it took a lot of willpower on my end, I managed to stay quiet. I did not tell him: "With all due respect, sir, my baby feeding devices are attached to me and it hasn't even been a week!" I didn't find the courage to get up and slam the door in his face. When I thought about it more that night, I didn't know what I should have done. I am still not sure. If it weren't for my coworkers, I would have regretted switching jobs a lot more.

No matter how difficult your journey is, whether it is in your personal life or professional, the people you are surrounded with will make a big difference in whatever you are facing. My peers, even the ones that didn't have little kids and couldn't really empathize, could see that I wasn't a slacker. I wasn't trying to break the rules or cheat the system. I was just a new mom who was extremely tired and wished her boss would cut her some slack, at least for the first couple of weeks.

In general, in the US, society does not place value, does not recognize the enormity, the impact pregnancy has on women. I won't go into details in this book, but when it comes to new moms, we mostly depend on the compassion and empathy of our bosses. Nobody owes anything to anyone. I have heard some arguments comparing the challenges related to motherhood to having aging parents, or pets, but there is a difference.

The new boss had a very old-school management style. He was so fixated on the hours worked, it seemed as though he didn't care about the actual outcomes delivered. This boss, who could use some coaching, ended up telling HR the following week that I come to work late and leave early. It was the most humiliating HR conversation I ever had. Looking back, I wonder why they didn't ask me at all how I was, they didn't congratulate me on my newborn baby. They just took his side. There was no empathy whatsoever. Knowing what I know now, I would probably use this as a coaching opportunity for both the HR and the boss, but back then, I was just a sleep-deprived young mom. The guy eventually was let go, but why didn't I walk away? Why didn't I quit the job, stay home with the baby, or find another job? Did I believe I had no choice?

I felt an obligation to stay because I made a promise to the hiring manager when I first joined. He wasn't even there anymore. I doubt he would care, but to me, it seemed like the right thing to do. I felt accountable because the company invested in me. They trained me for the full 6 months prior to my maternity leave and so I came back ready to work. I was afraid it wouldn't look good on my resume being at the job for under a year.

Something else was a factor in my decision to stay. Just six months earlier, my sister Ella had to make a similar decision. When she had her second baby, she only qualified for two weeks of paid maternity leave coverage. The first four weeks were unpaid, then she would get two weeks of reduced pay. She couldn't afford to stay home past that, so she planned to go back to work six weeks after having the baby. When the baby was three weeks old, she broke her wrist and she qualified to get a short-term disability for another six weeks. Eventually, she had to get back to work. She had a toddler, a newborn baby, and one functioning hand. Her husband was extremely supportive but that is beside the point. She went back to work and it was a nightmare. She lasted 3 months before giving up and quitting. Not sticking with it essentially killed her career. We didn't know back then the full extent of how that decision would impact her career. However, we knew that staying home full-time wasn't the right option for her and I know now it wouldn't have been the right option for me.

I hold no grudge, but the fact that I am writing about my first week of being back from maternity leave 15 years later means it clearly made an impact on me. One might say it traumatized me, but I say it made my skin thicker. It made me emotionally stronger and it made me more resilient.

It also made me more aware of the kind of manager I would NOT want to be. When the time came, I chose to be a manager that has empathy and compassion. I chose to not only help people grow professionally but made it a priority to also care about their families and their overall well-being.

> **PONDER:** If you are a boss, what kind of a boss are you? Do you only focus on the outcomes at work? Do you pay attention to a sustainable pace, making sure your employees work reasonable hours? What are your behaviors that contribute to the culture of your company?

As far as my sister goes, she found enough courage to pivot her career. She now holds a Doctorate Degree in Higher Education Administration and runs her own business.

We make our own choices in life. Sometimes they work out and sometimes we question them. Reflecting on those choices and learning from them helps. Regretting and dwelling on the fact that we should have done something different doesn't. Start from today. Think about tomorrow. Pivot. Create a new journey.

> **PONDER:** What does your today look like? What would you like your tomorrow to be?

When I became a manager for the first time with no managerial experience and not knowing what to do, I remembered one of my favorite managers, Joy, and followed her lead. One trait that made her so impactful is her giving a damn. She cared about our well-being, our families, and our careers. She had absolutely no ego and was willing to roll up her sleeves and do whatever it took, from work-related stuff to running out for an ice cream birthday cake to kitchen clean-up if that's what her team needed. That's leadership. I didn't know the term 'servant leadership' at the time, but I could recognize and appreciate the traits of a servant leader.

#MORECHUBAS TO SPREAD KINDNESS

Remember that boss who chose to make a new mother's life even more difficult rather than show a bit of compassion and perhaps even offer some additional support?

Well, imagine my surprise when I came back from my second maternity leave. A high-level executive named Chuba came over to congratulate me on the baby and asked how I was doing. We chatted for a bit and then he just offered his office if I ever needed it. He left it general, without specifying, but he was referring to me needing a place to pump milk. The office had a lock, shades on the door and it was across from my cube. I didn't know him for that long or that well. He had absolutely no idea what it meant to me after my experience with the boss after my first maternity leave. I appreciated it beyond what I could express with words. I didn't think of it then, but now as I am writing this book, I am thinking maybe I should start a new movement called, "More Chubas in our lives!"

He did something unexpected for me, something that he probably didn't even think was a big deal, but that moment of kindness and compassion stayed with me for over a decade now. Acts of kindness don't have to be big, expensive, or heroic. They can be simple. We can all look for an opportunity to be more kind.

HAVING THE COURAGE TO GIVE FEEDBACK

The first time I gave feedback, I was trembling from fear inside. The woman I was giving feedback to was in her 40s and I was 23. She was my colleague and we had to work side by side. As you know by now, I was raised in the former USSR. For the most part, we are very straight-forward people. Some of us have better filters than others, but the point is, we were raised with a "no bullshit" communication style. We often say it as it is. I don't know where I found the courage to give her the feedback I did, but it got to the point where I saw no other choice. I didn't know what she would say behind my back, but she was very inconsistent in her message to my face as far as my ability to get the job done and I was starting to lose sleep over it. She had this tendency to make me feel like I was the dumbest person.

We would troubleshoot something together and come across a piece of code that would basically just send a message out. What followed next was just a black box (in other words, messages would go over the wire) and so the next step in troubleshooting was to see if those messages were received on the other end. It makes perfect sense, except for the fact that I was barely out of school, so what seems super simple now, didn't seem simple then. I would ask a question and she would roll her eyes and often dismiss it. She wasn't an average engineer either. She was experienced and very smart, so I understand now how annoying it must have been for her to be stuck with me. I totally get it. While I acknowledge now that it could very well be my own leftover insecurities I described in previous chapters, I felt that if it continued, our working relationship would become even more toxic. I didn't expect her to mentor me, although I remember thinking that would have been great. The problem was that she was very inconsistent.

She would praise me in meetings one day and then completely disregard any troubleshooting suggestions or questions I had, clearly showing me that I didn't know much. This is what drove me crazy in our working relationship. If I would receive the same consistent message that I was dumb, I probably would just go on since it was a very familiar feeling to me. It is the whole praising part that was throwing me off. One day, I got enough courage to go over to her cube and ask if we could talk. I told her that I found it extremely difficult working with her. I shared with her that although all of this was easy for her, I just finished school

137

and what we were working on was all new to me. I asked her to either please stop praising me or to be my mentor and help. I was very nervous. She shared earlier that she had a very short fuse and couldn't always control her emotions, so I wasn't sure what to expect.

To my astonishment, she apologized to me. I didn't know what to expect, but I didn't expect an apology. Following that, this woman became one of the best mentors in my early career. From that point on, our relationship was based on honesty, empathy, and compassion.

> If we define compassion as "empathy plus action," then the following makes a lot of sense:
>
> **AWARENESS LEADS TO EMPATHY. EMPATHY LEADS TO COMPASSION. COMPASSION MEANS YOU TAKE ACTION. THAT ACTION COULD BE TO SPREAD KINDNESS. COMPASSION LEADS TO HEALTHY RELATIONSHIPS.**
>
> **HEALTHY RELATIONSHIPS LEAD TO A HEALTHY WORK ENVIRONMENT.**

When you become a subject matter expert, it is easy to think that your expertise is no big deal. It is important to be aware that not everyone starts from the same place that you are at. What might be easy for you might very well be the hardest thing someone else has ever done. It doesn't only apply to the technical world. It applies to all professions out there. It applies not only to the skills related to the job but also the mindset, the self-reflection, the awareness. Some people are great at the mechanics of their jobs but find it very difficult to give feedback in a way that yields healthy outcomes.

Look for an opportunity to help rather than blame or judge. Find the courage to give feedback. Help people be more self-aware since, as I stated above, awareness is the start of many great things. If you are in a leadership role, choose to lead with compassion.

I hope that I have shared enough in this book for the reader to think about their own lives and behaviors. Hopefully, this book can help the reader decide if there is anything they would like to improve.

FINDING COURAGE TO MAKE DECISIONS

Decision-making is difficult, especially if your decision may impact many people. Being afraid to be judged is another common cause for stalling. The paralysis on decision making may have different causes and the fear of making the wrong decision is often the root cause for the paralysis. How much data analysis is enough before making a decision? If you need to find the courage to make a difficult decision, think about what will happen if you don't make it. Think about the worst thing that could happen if you do make that decision. If you don't take action, progress doesn't happen.

I can go on and on...but I need to find the courage and make a decision to turn in a final manuscript of this book at some point...I can think of many reasons why I shouldn't publish this book (fear of people finding this book neither interesting nor valuable being one of the reasons) or I can think of at least one why I should. I choose progress over perfection. If this book helps at least one person, either in their personal life or professional, there is no reason to delay it. I choose to deliver value sooner rather than later.

In the summary table below, when it comes to the corporate world (my professional life), the reasons listed in the right column are why I have made a very scary decision to publish this book and include the corporate world aspect. Mindset and actions are everything. I choose to have courage, be open to feedback and continuously improve! I choose to share my life stories and my experience in hopes that it will bring as much value to as many people as possible!

IN SUMMARY

	T R A N S L A T E S TO	
Finding courage		Effective, loyal employees who are empowered to make decisions in a healthy work environment and not afraid to speak up.
Giving a damn		
Not blaming		
Not judging		They will thrive in a healthy work environment and hopefully see what they do daily not only as a job, but also as an opportunity to make friends for life and bring value to the customers.
Not pointing out negative personality traits behind someone's back (aka trashing someone)		
Feeding and Spreading kindness		They will take on challenging situations and, instead of blaming, look for a learning opportunity and continuous improvement.
Counting your blessings		
Building relationships		They will have self-awareness, ability to see different perspectives, and ability to adapt to change.
Being grateful		
Seeing different perspectives		They will find satisfaction in their work and they will have **a better chance of leading a *Life Worth Living!***
Having a positive outlook on life	→	

After being in the IT field since 1997, going from an individual contributor to leadership and now consulting, I concluded that having an open, healthy mindset is where any kind of initiative has a chance to start and survive. Without the ability to self-reflect and be open to continuously improve, we end up just moving pieces around without truly moving the needle. Our mindset, whether we are talking about personal life or professional, is the key between just existing and actually living *Lives Worth Living.*

If you had a magic wand and could make any change in your organization or yourself, what would you change?

_____

_____

_____

_____

_____

_____

_____

_____

_____

_____

_____

_____

CHAPTER 8

Finding your Purpose;
Creating Your Journey

"Every single one of us is entitled to feel fulfilled by the work we do, to wake up feeling inspired to go to work, to feel safe when we're there and to return home with a sense that we contributed to something larger than ourselves."
-SIMON SINEK, FIND YOUR WHY: A PRACTICAL GUIDE FOR DISCOVERING PURPOSE FOR YOU AND YOUR TEAM

There are some people who know at a young age exactly what they want to be when they grow up. They are the kind of people who have a five-year plan and have no problem articulating their life's vision when asked during an interview where they see themselves in x amount of years. Then, there is the kind of folks that have absolutely no idea what they want to do. They get their first job and see where it takes them. I don't think one kind is better than the other. I believe in planning and I believe in goals. I prefer, however, to not look too far ahead as I always found the "where do you see yourself in x years" question absurd. It sounds a bit judgmental, so let me rephrase it. I found it very challenging to answer. I know many people have goals in life and work all their life to achieve them. I admire that ability. I am also aware that it can lead to disappointment. What if earlier on in one's life, the goal that is set isn't the right goal? What if life throws a curveball at you and circumstances will not allow you to march towards that goal?

If you skipped all of the previous chapters, I will give you a summary. I share my life stories, as well as stories of my family to show that life is complex and unpredictable. Unexpected circumstances don't have to be as horrible as the start of a war. It could be deciding to stay home to raise a baby, which happens to derail your career. It could be cancer showing up at your doorsteps and in best-case scenarios just delaying your plans. Whatever it may be, the ability to pivot from your plan and sometimes even from your larger goal is a major skill of its own.

WHEN YOU HAVE NO CLUE, DO SOMETHING

As recent as two years ago when my boss asked what I wanted to do next, I had no idea. I debated for a couple of years if maybe an executive MBA could be the next thing but I wasn't sure what I wanted to do, so it seemed premature to go the MBA route. I decided at some point that doing something is better than nothing. I took an "Artificial Intelligence: Implications for Business Strategy" course at MIT and enjoyed it very much. It allowed me to have intelligent conversations and connect with people I otherwise would have nothing in common with. DOING SOMETHING is key here. Doing something that will bring some kind of value to you, your company or your customer is worth doing, even if you don't know for sure where it will lead.

In the corporate world, talking for hours and hours and hours without making any progress is something that I have very little patience for. If you don't know what you want or need to do, start with something small, learn from it and see where it takes you. It is possible that while you are working on something small, that next big idea will come to you in the process. The bottom line is, GET OFF YOUR ASS and DO SOMETHING! I know this sounds too straightforward and direct and might not sit well with everyone. I promise that if our paths cross and you let me know you find this way of communication offensive, I will not brush you off. When communicating with you, I will do my best to not use any offensive words, even if a nice swear word might be the best way to get a point across. With that being said, I have also learned over the years that there is no way one can please everyone and even though I still often try, I made peace with the fact that not everyone will like me or my style of communication. That is okay. I choose to chill. Life goes on.

GETTING RID OF THE IMPOSTER SYNDROME AND FINDING THAT NICHE

Full disclosure here, I am not a career or life coach. I am a digital transformation coach. I do sometimes lend an ear to friends and colleagues, and through some questions, help them either feel more confident in what they are doing or help them identify what that next step in their journey might look like.

I am happy to share my experience of how I got rid of the imposter syndrome and found what I truly enjoy. For those who never heard the term "imposter syndrome", it means you have a fear of people finding out that you are incompetent and that you don't belong in the role you are currently in. Don't get me wrong, when it comes to calling myself an "Author", I still very much have that syndrome. I know it will go away eventually. For now though, I am still in disbelief that I am about to become a published author.

When it comes to my earlier career as a software engineer, that's when that imposter syndrome would often kick in. I didn't learn that term until about seven years ago, but when I first heard it, I knew I had felt it on more than one occasion. It is not that I didn't like the job. I actually enjoyed coding very much. Feeling of getting your code to compile and watch it do what you wanted it to do was always extremely satisfying to me. The issue may have been that writing code wasn't my true passion. Teaching was. I wanted to be a teacher ever since I tutored a friend in my junior year of high school, helping her get an A in math and seeing that big smile on her face.

When I met my husband and he encouraged me to study computer science, I gave it a shot, mostly to see the respect and pride in his eyes. I am pretty sure I succeeded with that. It wasn't an easy journey for me. I was one of the very few females in the computer science program (glad to see more STEM programs for girls these days) and was surrounded by many guys who were passionate about computers. Many of them had been writing code since they were 10, encouraged by their very educated parents that had the means and access to those early computers they could pull apart and put back together. In comparison, I had access to computers in a computer lab. When my very first boss asked me to shut down my PC on my way out, I had no clue what he wanted me to do as if he said it in some foreign language. I am not kidding. It was very embarrassing, to say the least.

When it came to my master's degree in computer science, I did it because the company I worked for was paying for it. I found a way to enroll without having to take the graduate school entrance exam and it just seemed like the next logical thing to do. I didn't have a five-year plan and didn't know what I would use the master's in computer science for, but I knew it wouldn't hurt. I enjoyed people's reactions when I would share I was working on my master's degree. It had a good ring to it. I don't know if it made me a better engineer, but there is something about that piece of paper that gets you certain respect without having to prove yourself, at least at the beginning of a career. No matter how successful I was at my jobs, I never felt anything but average. I often felt that soon enough, someone would be on to me and would figure out that I was not really a software engineer. That was the imposter syndrome talking. In reality, I was told by many that my technical knowledge and

146

ability to get work done was above average. I never had bad reviews and so far, nobody came forward to let me know they couldn't stand working with me. Huge WIN!

When I became a Scrum Master and then an Agile Coach, I noticed I didn't have to work extra hard to be good. It just came naturally to me, as if that role was created just for me. Going to work was like a holiday every day. When my new role put me in front of a crowd with a microphone in my hand, my hands didn't tremble and my voice didn't crack. It was fun. When my role took me on the road, flying domestically and internationally where I met hundreds of new people each year, it gave me a thrill! Getting up at 3:30 am to catch a 6 am flight was not a bother. Seeing my coworkers at 5 am at Logan Airport put a huge smile on my face, regardless of how tired I may have been. That's when I started reading more and more about neurological communication and social styles and connected my preference to meet and interact with people to the jobs that might be more suitable for me.

I came to realize that my passion for teaching was still there. It is actually the reason I taught skiing in the winter for many years. Running training sessions and interactive workshops, watching people have those "aha" moments brings me a lot of joy. Sitting in long meetings for ten hours a day doesn't. Studying computer science for so many years and working as a software engineer earned me certain respect and ability to find a common language with many roles within an IT organization. It gave me the skills to sit through long meetings if I need to. It is nice to have a choice not to though!

The concept of choosing the lifestyle you want and then choosing a profession that will allow you to have that lifestyle sounded very appealing to me. They didn't teach that in school when I was studying. You don't go to medical school if you want to work from the ski slopes or the beach. If you are a software engineer but you love traveling, you can look for a large software company with offices all over the world. That might give you an opportunity to travel for work. If you are an introvert and meeting new people exhausts you, you probably don't want to be a Product Manager or a salesperson. Not to say that you couldn't if you decided for yourself that that was your goal. Introvert just means you prefer to keep to yourself, but it doesn't mean that you couldn't become an extrovert if it was aligned with whatever you decided you wanted to do. Agile or Digital Transformation coaching is probably not the best choice if you don't want to connect with people. You have to love people in that coaching role! If not love, then at least tolerate! I am kidding...well, actually, I am not. If you don't enjoy interacting with people and that desire to help doesn't come naturally to you, I am pretty sure coaching won't bring you much joy.

What I also learned along the way is that no matter what you choose to do, even if it is not your thing at the moment, there is a good chance you are still getting the skills and experience that will not be wasted and might potentially lead you to something that will be more suitable for you. You may want to find a good mentor, have a conversation with someone similar in personality and/or interests as you. Another option is to read books or listen to podcasts. I was extremely lucky to have a few people in my life who saw the skills and personality traits in me I didn't realize I had (Thank you Oleg Vitsev!). Their encouragement, sometimes persuasion, to take on a new role when I didn't think I was qualified enough led me to my current path; the path that got rid of the imposter syndrome, and that brings me a lot of joy every single day!

PONDER: What is it that you always wanted to do but haven't gotten a chance to try yet? What are the obstacles? What is the smallest thing you could do now that would eventually get you closer to your goal? Who could you ask for advice or help? What WILL you do as the first step?

WHY DID I WRITE THE BOOK?

Writing this book was not really part of anything I thought I had to do in order to move a needle in my transformation or my career. It started as part of something I wanted to do to get my mind occupied while my daughter was going through chemo and I had to stay strong. Losing many people in my life and seeing cancer affecting so many people around me, I couldn't help but think, *What legacy will I leave behind when it is my time to go? Will my life and my family stories fade away in my kids' memories just like I am starting to lose whatever my grandparents have shared with me when I was younger?* It morphed into a book on resilience and a positive outlook on life gradually as I was writing.

The process of writing this book wasn't only educational for me, it allowed me to connect with my family, especially with my sister, on a much deeper level. Our perspectives on our family situation were very different. Reflecting on our family story was healing for both of us. I don't know where writing this book will take me but I am glad that I ACTUALLY WROTE IT!!!

I hope this book will help people find courage, be more compassionate, encourage them to self-reflect, heal and give them more confidence in whatever it is they would like to accomplish. I hope this book will inspire them to take that next step in creating their own journey and finding their purpose. I encourage the reader to ponder and find something that would make their lives, a *Life Worth Living*!

Conclusion

On September 15th, 2020, about 4 months since I decided to write the memoir, this conclusion was the only thing left to write. At 2:05 pm, I had one of the biggest meltdowns of my life. I am talking about uncontrollable crying, with crocodile tears which lasted no less than a half an hour. I was sitting in my basement office trying to get myself together before my next meeting.

Why am I sharing this vulnerable moment as a conclusion of the book on resilience? That is because we are all human and we all have our limits. There is a time and a place where we have to be strong and when we can afford to let go.

When kids are born, the most heartwarming words to hear are, "You have a healthy baby. Your baby is perfect." When kids (regardless of their age) get sick, you desperately want to hear they will be ok. They are not always ok. Some journeys are harder than others. In many cases, the journeys do not have a happy ending, but in my case, to my relief, it did!

A few minutes before my breakdown, I got a call from my daughter's oncologist. What I heard next was the best words a parent could hear, "It is official! Scans looked good. No more cancer. No more treatment!"

There isn't really much more to say...I shared my life up until today. I shared how I focus on problems at hand, putting emotions aside until the problem is resolved. I shared how I cope in most difficult situations and manage to throw punches back at whatever life decides to throw at me.

I shared my journey of building resilience in the hopes that it helps you to find yours!

About the Author

Luba Sakharuk was born in Vilnius, Lithuania in 1978. She settled in Boston, Massachusetts with her mother and sister on September 30th, 1992 and graduated from Brookline High School in 1996. After overcoming many challenges as an immigrant, without much financial support, not speaking English, and in her case, also tremendously missing her father who stayed behind in Lithuania, she was accepted into Northeastern University where she received an undergraduate degree in computer science. While working full time as a software engineer, she continued her studies and graduated from Worcester Polytech Institute of Technology in 2004 with a master's degree in computer science with a concentration in computer and communication network. Luba took a bit of a break from formal studies to raise two daughters but she never took a break from working or learning. Her career led her to agile coaching, leadership and now digital transformations. Her passion for solving engineering and business problems led her to MIT Sloan Executive Education and, eventually, to becoming a published author.

Her passion has always been teaching and mentoring, so when she didn't spend time in the corporate world, she could be found on the ski slopes of Loon Mountain teaching people of all ages the art of downhill skiing.

Besides skiing, Luba taught various aspects of business and process related frameworks over the years. After being in the IT field since 1997, she came to a realization that having a positive outlook on life and an ability to embrace change is essential for whatever one wants to accomplish, whether it is becoming a better skier or transforming large organizations. Our mindset is critical in our choice between just existing and actually living Lives Worth Living.

Acknowledgement

I would like to thank Nat, Stu, Vivi and the rest of the Ultimate 48 Hour Author team for being there from day one of this journey. Their expertise exceeded all expectations and I will be forever grateful for their coaching.

I would like thank my family for their support, their willingness to relive painful memories and in the case of my sister Ella, countless iterations of editing and honest feedback.

I would like to thank my friends for many conversations where I am sure I talked about this book more than I should have but they listened patiently and often with interest!

I would like to thank my uncle Valera, and my friends Anna Ortiz, Aliona Tchumanov and Irina Ganopolsky for taking on the role of beta readers and providing me invaluable suggestions.

I would like to thank my friend Ilona Gluzman for translating sections of the book to Russian for my family in Russia.

I would like to thank my cousin Yael for reading the first few chapters early on in the process and confirming the content made sense and was correct.

I would like to thank my husband for not only supporting me in the effort of writing this memoir, but also sharing his story, having to also relive the painful times we often want to forget.

Lastly, I would like to thank my beautiful girls for being my biggest inspiration! Being a mom has been and always will be my greatest joy and achievement in life!

**Luba with daughters, Anna and Elena!
The greatest joy and achievement in life!**

Calls to Action

"The delicate balance of mentoring someone is not creating them in your own image, but giving them the opportunity to create themselves."

—STEVEN SPIELBERG

I thought a lot about whether to include any exercises in this book on not. I am not a doctor, so I haven't done any of the research myself. I have read enough books to know there is definitely science behind what has worked for me and I list a few of the books I read later in this chapter. I have shared my life story and lessons learned. The following is what helps me stay calm, have a positive outlook on life, be resilient and feel good about the life I am living,

- Asking myself the PONDER questions, analyzing my life situations, and looking at all I am facing or have faced from different perspectives.
- I found actively looking for the good to be very effective.
- Having someone to talk it through helps tremendously. In my case, it was mostly my sister and my uncle, but I had many others that I shared my ideas with.

If you would like a FREE **PONDER JOURNAL,** you can request it via the subscription form on my website, **www.lubasakharuk.com**

- Making a financial contribution to a charity affects my happiness. This year was definitely all about cancer research and I was grateful to be employed and be in a position to support everyone I knew who participated in the Pan-Mass Challenge (PMC).
- I find joy in giving back. It doesn't have to be financial. I give my time. The most precious gift of all. I joined career coaching groups to help people looking for a career changing advice. I make time to listen to people. I connect people and I connect with people.
- As much as possible, I try to support those who are struggling with keeping their businesses afloat by simply commenting on LinkedIn to show support or sharing their posts to spread the awareness. It doesn't cost anything and it brings value.

The Pan-Mass Challenge (PMC) is a fundraising bike-a-thon started in 1980 by Billy Starr to benefit the Dana-Farber Cancer Institute via the Jimmy Fund. It raises more money than any other single athletic fundraiser in the country.

You can donate directly to Dana Farber at, https://www.dana-farber.org/how-you-can-help/ways-to-give/

For those who truly want to make a change in their outlook on life or just simply need a little help with someone holding them accountable, I highly recommend working with a coach or a mentor. Transformations aren't easy, neither personal nor corporate.

With that said, there is a lot of information available on this topic and many books written. It feels counterproductive to recreate it in this book. The following two books have many references to research done by psychiatrists, psychologists, and neuroscientists that make convincing the audience that rewiring your brain is possible. They both also list very specific step by step instructions for certain exercises.

> **BOOKS:**
>
> *Personality Isn't Permanent* by Benjamin Hardy, PhD.
>
> *The Source* by Tara Swart, Md, PhD.

Among many others, **JOURNALING** is listed as a proven technique in many books written by credible people with credible degrees.

As long as you **DO SOMETHING**, you will get closer to the outcome you are trying to achieve!

I wish you the best of luck on your journey!

If you are looking for a sounding board and would like to connect with people who have read this book, there is a dedicated **Facebook Fan Page** called **"Create Your Journey; Life Worth Living"** with the following description,

"The purpose of this page is to create space for people who would like to discuss the book, *Life Worth Living* and share their experiences and journeys. This space is for those who would like to inspire others as well as those looking to be inspired!"

If you have any questions, my email is **luba@lubasakharuk.com**

> **"We make a living by what we get, but we make a life by what we give."**
>
> **–WINSTON CHURCHILL**

LUBA SAKHARUK

Luba Sakharuk has always wanted to live a Life Worth Living. After coming to the US from Vilnius, Lithuania in 1992 and graduating from Brookline High School, she was accepted into Northeastern University where she earned an undergraduate degree in computer science and has worked in the IT industry for over 20 years.

Her career led her to agile coaching, professional facilitation, leadership and digital transformations. Her passion for solving engineering and business problems steered her towards a master's degree in computer science from Worcester Polytech Institute of Technology, MIT Sloan Executive Education and, eventually, to becoming a published author.

Throughout her life, Luba has always been teaching, mentoring and sharing her knowledge and expertise with others to inspire and empower. She has been interviewed by O'Reilly, appeared in various podcasts and facilitated hundreds of powerful workshops.

A highly engaging and inspiring presenter, Luba has spoken on her career journey, and various other topics at events such as "She Geeks out", "Women in Technology", as well as Lunch and Learn Programs and various other events, all focused on inspiring attendees to self-reflect on their own journeys and guide them towards that next step.

Able to adapt her presentations between 30 minutes to a full day program, Luba's 3 main keynotes are:

Creating your own Journey to a Life Worth Living

- ✓ How to Banish Impostor Syndrome
- ✓ How to get Unstuck
- ✓ How to hold yourself Accountable

Overcoming any Challenge Life Throws at You

- ✓ How to find Courage
- ✓ How to go from Blaming to Healing
- ✓ How to find Happiness

Breakthrough Lies Beyond the Comfort Zone

- ✓ How to embrace Change
- ✓ How to get a Buy in
- ✓ How to minimize Stress

To engage Luba to speak at your next event, email luba@lubasakharuk.com for pricing and availabilities.

WWW.LUBASAKHARUK.COM

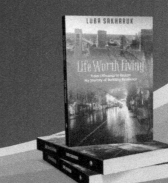

Notes

CPSIA information can be obtained
at www.ICGtesting.com
Printed in the USA
FSHW010916131120